LETTERS TO MY
YOUNGER SELF

LETTERS TO MY YOUNGER SELF

An Anthology of Writings by
Incarcerated Men at S.C.I.
Graterford and a Writing
Workbook

Edited by Jayne Thompson
and Emily DeFreitas
Afterword by Thomas E. Kennedy

SERVING HOUSE BOOKS

ISBN: 978-0-9913281-0-9

Cover by Les Herman (www.leslieherman.com)
Serving House Books logo by Barry Lereng Wilmon

Published by Serving House Books, LLC
Copenhagen, Denmark and Florham Park, NJ
www.servinghousebooks.com
Member of The Independent Book Publishers Association

First Serving House Books edition 2014

"The Purpose of Poetry," from *After the Rain*, by Jared Carter used with kind permission of the author.

"Two Dogs" by Charles Simic, used with kind permission of the author.

William Stafford, "Traveling through the Dark" from *The Way It Is: New and Selected Poems*. Copyright 1998 by the Estate of William Stafford. Reprinted with the permission of The Permissions Company, Inc. on behalf of Graywolf Press, Minneapolis, Minnesota www.graywolf.com

Afterword: Thomas E Kennedy, "Humanitarians at the Grate: The Writing Group at Graterford Maximum Security Prison," was originally published in the May-Summer 2013 issue of *The Writer's Chronicle*, the journal of the Association of Writers and Writing Programs (AWP)

TABLE OF CONTENTS

FAMILY

A CONVERSATION WITH A POET

Creative Responses

AFTERWORD

This book is dedicated to
FRANK TURNER
(December 29, 1995-October 17, 2013),
a kind and intelligent young man who was murdered in Chester, PA.
We hope this book will reach out to youths like Frank and his killer
to prevent further loss and suffering.

SPECIAL THANKS

We are very appreciative of Les Herman (www.leslieherman.com) for allowing us to use his art work on the cover and for designing the front cover of this book.

Marty Flowers gave these pages a thorough proofreading and editorial review, and we are grateful for her contribution.

A special thank you goes out to family and friends who have advised me on this project: Margaret Taggart, Linda Jacobson, James Ervin, Robin Fletcher, Jeanine Rastatter, Tamme Hoey, Tina George, Al Brophy. In addition, I must thank Jackie Scharff for listening and offering her advice on the project. Alice Schell, a.k.a. Violet, has given me years of friendship and countless hours of advice. She has supported this project in so many ways.

A NOTE ABOUT NAMES

Pennsylvania prison administrators requested that the editors not identify anthology contributors out of concern and respect for crime victims. Therefore, with the authors' permission, we replaced their last names with only their last initial.

Paul J. P.

LEARN FROM OUR MISTAKES, YOUNG MEN AND WOMEN, YOU CAN HAVE A BEAUTIFUL FUTURE!

Most of the men in our writing group at Graterford maximum security prison have been incarcerated 10, 20, or 30 plus years. Professor Jayne Thompson invited us to share some of our writing with the juvenile offenders – youth at real risk of winding up with long-term prison sentences – through her Restorative Justice volunteer work in Chester, Pa. We all thought it was an excellent idea and an opportunity to do a real service to the community we had come from.

Through media and personal experience, we have spent decades witnessing the senseless street crime and violence devastating our communities. Probably more than half of our group members have been actively involved in organized prison reform, social justice, or public safety endeavors for years. Naturally, we saw sharing our stories with at-risk youth as a unique opportunity to potentially salvage the futures of youth who might learn from our mistakes.

And it is clear that the publication of this book of our experiences before we went to prison and the mistakes we made would reach a wider audience of "Jayne's Juvies." Under the tutelage of Professor Jayne Thompson, this is the book conceived and created by the men in the 2011 Prison Literacy Program Creative Writing Class at Graterford Prison.

> We broke the code of cool
> By undressing our souls,
> Discarding robes
> Of vanity and pride.
> With aging bodies entombed
> Like pyramid mummies,

9

Our crippled spirits limp
Along the winding path
To redemption.
We write wrongs to mentor youth
And redeem our souls.

We hope that you young men and women might read these stories of broken lives which have been reconstructed in words and stories and memories and that they might inspire you to explore your minds and your hearts and your dreams and make a turn away from the loss of your freedom and save yourselves for the potentially beautiful lives that are open to you.

Jayne Thompson

INTRODUCTION

This summer, I taught in a program for youths in Chester, Pennsylvania, a small city facing the problems of poverty. While discussing West Virginia coal miners in Diane Gilliam Fisher's *Kettle Bottom*, one young woman of fifteen spoke up: "It's like a prison. The men are shackled to the mine like men in prison." We began discussing prisons, and the students explained that some of them had been mandated by courts to be in the summer program, a few had spent time in a juvenile detention center, others had a family member or knew someone in prison, and some were afraid of prison and those in it. One young man asked, "Do you believe that people can change?" His eyes, dark and round, begged me to say, "Yes." I said, "Absolutely. I have seen it happen." After class I thought about it; yes, I believe people can change, but perhaps it is more a matter of people choosing to tap into what Abraham Lincoln called "the better angels of our nature." The good is always in us, and we choose it—or not.

Over the past three years of teaching creative writing for the Prison Literacy Project at S.C.I. Graterford, I have met many men who work hard to nourish these "better angels," and do so while serving a prison sentence, some of them, for life. At Graterford, I talked about the Youth Aid Panel I serve on in Chester where I hear the cases of juvenile offenders. The panel listens to the children and tries to determine a resolution for the offense. He or she returns with the resolution completed, and the criminal record is expunged. The child can come before us only once; after that, he or she goes into the court system. I had wished on so many occasions that these young people could meet the Graterford guys and hear their stories and wisdom. This anthology is that wish realized. The anthology contributors wrote pieces about regretful decisions made or painful experiences in their youth, fearlessly exposing their vulnerability. The men chose many methods for sharing their messages; some wrote letters to their young selves or family members, telling of their struggles growing up in difficult circumstances. Others wrote responses to poems with a particular prompt in mind, forming a conversation with a famous poet. Other pieces discuss making good decisions and finding a safe place in which to grow up.

The Graterford writing group reached out from behind the prison walls to speak to young people, but they speak to us all. They remind us all about choices, consequences, and caring for others. Their courage is remarkable as they ask themselves and readers to make better decisions and work toward a more compassionate world; in short, they ask us to tap into those "better angels."

Suggestions for Writing

We hope that the "Suggestions for Writing" in each of the four central sections of this book might serve as an inspiration to conjure up in the young men and women those "better angels" and reflect on and write about them in addressing ourselves and in decisions that affect us, our homes, our families and the poetry of our lives.

Emily DeFreitas

A Word from the Typist

I once thought I shoplifted by accident, if that's even possible. I immediately freaked out and told my mother, who showed me the receipt. She had paid for the bubble gum, or lollipop, or barrette. I don't even remember what it was. That's as close as I've ever been to crime in my life (unless speeding occasionally counts), and I always assumed that people who commit crime must be crazy. I do not think that anymore.

After reading, typing, and thinking about the pieces by these writers, I can't ignore the fact that these people, unlike the easily labeled "bad guys" on TV, are real. They had real life experiences that led them to the lives they lived before prison, and the experiences they have now are just as real. As a 19-year-old college student, I respect them for their experience. But I also respect them for their courage to share this experience in writing. Today, after reading their work, I am surprised but not ashamed to say that I wish I knew these writers. I wish everyone could hear the stories Professor Thompson told me about meeting with them, and read all the pieces that didn't make it into this book. I never thought I'd work on a project like this, but I'm glad I did.

Jayne Thompson

ACKNOWLEDGMENTS

I will be forever grateful to Serving House Books for publishing this volume and for volunteering to publish it without financial profit. Any profits from the sale of this book go into printing other copies to be distributed to young people free of charge. The publishers, Thomas E. Kennedy and Walter Cummins, have also sent donated books to the Graterford guys, and Tom Kennedy, after donating copies of his novel, *In the Company of Angels*, visited the men to give a reading and talk with them about writing, one of the most memorable nights of my three years at Graterford.

I could not have completed this project without the help of my co-editor, Emily DeFreitas, an undergraduate English and creative writing student at Widener University with a heart as large as her mind. She was a source of inspiration and constant joy as we made difficult choices on which pieces worked in the collection and created suggestions for writing. Not to mention that every piece had to be typed!

I am also grateful to the secretary of the Widener Humanities Department, Beth Homan, who took pity on me, and in her own free time, typed pieces for the book. In addition, she listened to all my worries and helped me think through problems.

The Center for Resolutions in Media, Pennsylvania, has taught me so much about conflict resolution and restorative justice. My hope is that this book reaches great numbers of young people through their various programs, including Youth Aid Panels.

S.C.I. Graterford opened its doors to me and allowed me to bring in books and teaching materials to the men. I cannot thank the administration enough.

A special thank you goes to Paul P. He asked me to come to Graterford to teach the class and helped me in so many ways to understand how to teach a class in a prison. Paul Vergalla, a librarian at Graterford, and Razzaqq G., a contributor to this book, have been very supportive in helping me in the final stages of this book.

The class and the project could not have happened without Robert Bender, the newly retired head of the Prison Literacy Project. He is an extraordinary man who worked tirelessly to spread his great love of literature through the prison. We all thank him.

Dr. Lori Pompa, the director of the Inside/Out Prison Program, wrote a letter of support of my teaching at the prison. She also trained me well in following prison regulations and running a classroom.

I received much assistance from Widener University faculty and students. Dr. Kenneth Pobo and the members of his poetry writing class; Dr. Michael Cocchiarale; Prof. Brenda Wolfer; Dr. Patricia Dyer; Dr. Mara Parker; Samuel Starnes; Trudy Depew; Chara Kramer, a Widener student who edited a few essays for the book and wrote an article about the project; Jillian Benedict, a Widener student who edited a few pieces; Prof. James Esch; Dr. Janine Utell, Chair of English; and Dr. Mark Graybill, Associate Dean of Humanities. Thank you all.

The men in the Graterford creative writing class gave their time, talent, and personal stories to this project. They drafted and redrafted, created suggestions for writing assignments, and supported me through the process. My life has been forever enriched by my time teaching at Graterford. I am so thankful to all who made it possible and all the men who took the class and taught me so much.

LETTERS

Christopher R. W. M.

God Bless!

Dear Christopher,

I know that it's still 1968, and you're five years old, but I need to discuss some things with you. Some issues that might quiet your fears, give you relief, and bring peace to your juvenile mind. I know that this may sound unbelievable, but my name is Christopher, and I'm you—forty-three years in the future.

I also know that you're scared of your older sibling because he abuses you. I know that you went to school today with a busted lip and a black eye that your sibling gave you. When the teachers and principal asked you what had happened, you remained silent. I know how much you love your sister and hate your sibling. I'm pleased to say that your hate is changing in the present day to forgiveness and empathy and, yes, even a simmering of love for him.

Empathy is a word that is used meaning to "feel" what another person might be experiencing both emotionally and mentally. I know that such a word or concept may seem foreign to you—because people in the neighborhood seem to cast a blind eye at your cuts, swollen eyes, busted lips, sprained limbs, and other injuries that a little child shouldn't have to go through—but I believe, deep down inside, the neighbors honestly care for you.

Child abuse—this is what it's called. It wasn't defined back in your time, but it's big business now. Do you know that today if a child calls the police and says that his parents beat him very badly, he could have them arrested and thrown into prison? The child could possibly even be taken to a safe home where he could have new adults that love and support him. I bet that got you thinking, huh?

I know, despite your abuse, you have no concept of death. I often wished I was dead when I was your age. Remember the night when our sibling abused us **very** badly, and we went to the kitchen and tried to cut our wrist with a butcher knife? I remember how hopeless we felt and afterwards we prayed to God to take us away from the family that we live with and give us new siblings. When we didn't hear God's voice answer us back, we prayed to Satan for the same thing, and told the devil that we would let him take over our body if he helped us. We were real desperate then, weren't we?

I guess you're wondering why I'm writing to you when you're five years old. I wanted to tell you that despite the abuse you're going through, regardless of the bullies that you're going to deal with, and even with the debased people that use your body for their sinful lusts, there **is hope,** Christopher.

I know that people seem like they don't love you, and that you'd just like a hug every now and then, or a reward for getting good grades in school—this will come to you in about five more years when you're eleven years old and in sixth grade. I know that this seems like an eternity, but it'll come—I'm forty-eight years old now, aren't I? By the way, I still have your future sixth grade teacher's phone number (Miss Heath)—she's the one person that will take an interest in you—showing you the love that you crave. I can honestly say that I value your inner strengths, your devotion to family, and your desire to befriend and protect the helpless, Christopher. I love you deeply, profoundly, and yes, without expecting anything in return.

I want you to know, despite all that you're currently going through emotionally, physically, and mentally, there are good people in this world—yes, even right where you live. I know how observant you are—if you look hard enough, you'll see the love and concern in your neighbors' eyes—they're just as frightened, abused, lonely, and hurt as you're feeling right now, Christopher.

I was thinking what advice I could give you that would make an impact on your life. Remember our hiding place when people used to abuse us? That dark hole buried in the earth under our yard in the basement—where even the rats were afraid to go? I want to tell you not to run and hide in there anymore. OK? Do you know that I still hide in the dark when I'm feeling sad or hurt? It's a bad habit, hiding in the dark, Christopher, and one that we carried with us forty-three years later.

Well, I will end for now and save this letter for you inside a cell wall panel—that's right. Because we couldn't express our pain and torment, we wound up spending some time in jail. I won't tell you how much time we currently have inside this place, but after being here for a while, we eventually grew into the man that our mother and grandfather always wanted us to be. I want you to start opening up to people, Christopher. Tell them your story, how horrible your home life is, and how fearful it is to go to bed at night, how often you stay up at night listening for the door latch to turn and feel a hot, unwanted body lay next to yours.

Be strong, Christopher. Get your full education, and become a success to prove all those people wrong that said you'd never amount to anything. Life is too short, my little self, make good use of it. OK? I love you so very, very much. I always will.

Affectionately,
Your future self,

Christopher

James T.

James,

 I want to share something with you about yourself that, if taken the right way, could greatly benefit you.

 I'm aware of the emotional problem you've been struggling with since kindergarten. Somehow you got it into your head that you were dumb and ugly, and that people wouldn't like you because of that. That's why you were always so shy and quiet in school. You didn't socialize with your classmates as much as you should, not because you didn't want to, but because you were afraid of being rejected and hurt. As a result you sat off alone in painful isolation, afraid to join in as other children played all around you. That's why Miss Patterson, the kindergarten teacher, gave you the note that time for your mother. It said, "James is a good boy, but he needs to learn how to play with the other children."

 Being overly self-conscious of your perceived shortcomings, you dreaded being called on in class. Too many times you were made to look foolish and were snickered at when you couldn't get the answer right. Because of the problems you were experiencing, you lost interest in school early on.

 Being turned off to education, you got through school basically for just showing up. In tenth grade, when you were old enough, you quit school. By then you had taken to the streets full time. Hanging out with other drop-outs, you adopted a wayward lifestyle that had no worthwhile purpose or future to look forward to other than one beset with trouble, violence, prison or death. Trapped in idleness with an excessive desire for pleasure seeking, you exposed yourself to drugs, alcohol, crime, partying and having unprotected sex as a badge of honor with different females of like nature.

 James, you've got to learn what it takes to give yourself a chance in life while there's still time. And you've got to get rid of those negative, false and misleading feelings about yourself that fool you into believing the fake masks of characters you think people admire.

Do you know what I think tough is, James? Tough is learning how to ask for help when it really counts most in your life. That's what real toughness is. And it takes real courage to love yourself that much to be that tough. It's easy to be a loser and take the easy way out through a loser's lifestyle.

It is ironic, James, that it would be at Holmesberg Prison, at age 29, that you'd heed a lesson from your past to serve you in a time of dire need. The prison had just experienced the stabbing deaths of its warden and deputy warden by radical inmates. Playing on that violent situation, a copy-cat inmate, posing as a revolutionary Black Nationalist, tried to intimidate you into becoming part of a gang he had formed to do his bidding. Already in deep trouble, in a strange city, and charged with murder with no help, you wanted no part of it. No way were you going to submit yourself to more trouble brought into your life from the actions of someone else.

When this inmate ordered you to fall in line for drill exercises, you heard voices from the past admonishing you when you were being smacked around and talked down to in similar situations. "Don't let people mistreat you and talk to you in any kind of way. Stand up for yourself. You'd be a fool not to."

You refused this inmate's command and stood your ground. There would be no going to the guards for protection or seeking help from other inmates. You would confront the situation on your own in defense of yourself in order to break free, no longer holding back. Confident, adrenaline surging in your body at a high pitch, you were prepared to do battle and live with the consequences.

Although he was twice your size, you were not afraid of him. It registered in your body. Sensing that he would lose if he came at you, he backed off. And it was from that one determined incident that you experienced the power of loving yourself enough to break free of other people's bullshit.

My advice to you is that you reach out to someone you respect and trust that you can talk to. Someone like your mother, father, a relative, a religious person or an older person who cares. I don't care what's going on in your life, reaching out to any of those people, letting them know of the things you're struggling with is the best thing you could do for yourself. Don't be afraid to say what's on your mind. Trust me, that would build confidence and start to get you to a place you need to be to turn your life around.

A mentor, even now, especially now, could help motivate you toward school again and getting that diploma and moving on to the next level.

I hope you're giving serious thought to this. It is the one thing I wished deep down inside: that someone had stepped in to help me at your age. Taking such advice could turn your life around 180 degrees. Finding your way to the Creator would turn it 360 degrees. That is the potential I see for you.

How do I know? Because I <u>am</u> you, that same hurt and confused little boy, now 65 years later as a grown man in prison serving a life sentence, reaching back in time to <u>you</u> to help save <u>you</u> from a similar fate.

James, you can start to reclaim your life from where you are right now. **<u>Educate</u>** yourself at all cost. Scream for help where it hurts most if you must. Humanity will respond if you're sincere.

Trust me.

Michael W.

Dear young Michael,

When I first came to jail, I was having fun. I didn't care about anything, not even my own life. I was still in my stuck up ways because I was sixteen. Nothing mattered to me. I was robbing people, running into people's cells and taking what I wanted. So basically I wasn't learning anything. It was my way or no way. I wasn't going to school most of the time, but when I went I was a problem. None of the staff liked me, but they all respected me. I stabbed people and got stabbed. I fought guards and inmates. I won and lost fights, but that's what made me the man I am today. I have been in prison since I was sixteen. Now I'm 25. That's nine years straight without being able to touch my loved ones, see my loved ones. I can't leave and go to the store when I want, I don't have my freedom, and I have been told what to do for nine years. I only just started getting my life together once I got away from people my own age.

When I came to Graterford, my life changed forever. I'm not glorifying jail, but I can honestly say that without my coming to Graterford I would not have changed. Being around a bunch of old heads and listening to their life stories and all the mistakes they made in their lives helped me to change. Then I listened to all the different ways of how they changed their lives. Then there's all the opportunity that Graterford has to offer. All the vocational trades and programs. They taught me the things I know about life.

Being away from my family, however, made me appreciate my freedom a lot more. I can't imagine being away from them for another nine years. I did some things in my life that I'm not proud of. I always said that can't no old head teach me nothing and that no person in jail can teach me, but as I grew so did my love and respect for those older than me.

Jail is no place to be and it shouldn't have taken my coming here for me to change, so to all reading this, take heed of the message behind it. I was ya'll age doing and living the same life.

Please listen.

FROM: **Charles K. D.**

TO: Self

When I was 16 I had a great girlfriend. Her name was Margo. In my mind she was the sweetest person I ever met.

Now that I am 61 years young, I think of her words often. On more than one occasion, she suggested that I stay home with her. Her words always suggested that there was nothing good in hanging out with the crowd.

Do you remember that?

It seems to come back in my mind when I am speaking with my own son.

Why do you think her words keep ringing in your mind?

I can see now that there is a message in those words. They apply today as much as they did 45 years ago.

Would you agree that the moral of that experience represents the need to keep good company? I understand today that she was the one person who truly had my interest above all else. She was not trying to be selfish, but her motherly nature was alive and well.

Young men should cleave to the womb that birthed them, and apply common sense when judging whom to listen to. Women have an ability to see further than men can see.

Son, take note that more of us men are in the graveyard because when their wives, women, mothers told them to stay home on that night—we did not listen.

Not all, but *some* women have the sense of the womb that is the source of life. When you meet such a woman—be it mother, sister, or sweetheart—listen to her.

Young man, learn to listen to the heart and the soul of the women who love you. Remember, young man, women are in your arms to bring you love and comfort. Love does not lie. Listen to it, and you will become a better man, and a happy person. Listen to her, and be patient with her, and you will see that all that you attempt to achieve will happen for both of you.

Don't let your Margo get away.

D. Saadiq P.

Donny,

What's up, Big Guy!

Listen, I've been hearing a lot of things lately, some good and some bad!

You're 15 years old now and you have grown into a man's body so people are receiving you as an adult, but you are still a kid. I want to ask you something.

What do you want to be? What do you want to do from this point on? What are your goals?

You're good at basketball, great at track and even better with the clippers. So what do you want out of life, because with all of your abilities you still have to put in the work. Things are not always going to come easy for you, you know?

You've just come home from the Gabe's and now you're going to De La Salle. I know about the records you broke in track up the Gabe's along with getting good grades and winning the championship in basketball. But now you're home and going to school, and you're still doing the same shit!

Dig this, I know you like the lure of the streets. The girls, the cars and the clothes, but the things that you're doing ain't gonna do nothing but cause you to lose all that shit, cuz ain't no girls, cars, and clothes in the penitentiary.

Yeah, I know you're smarter than the next man and got all the answers, but think about this. How hard is it to transfer the time and energy you waste in the streets to the basketball court or the track?

See, your fucking problem is you look like a man but don't think like one, because a man don't do the silly shit you do, like beat a nigga up for his jacket on the EL train just so your homie can have one like yours. I know, I know. You got away with it, but what if you didn't? You would have been jammed up for moving out for somebody else! Let that nigga get his own money and buy a butter and some glasses like you did.

Think, man, use your head. You have a job at the Chart House. You worked for that bread. You didn't get it standing on the corner. You worked after school and on the weekends, saved your money and paid for that shit. Let them niggas work for theirs like you did!

You know as I write this letter to you, I feel like I'm wasting my time and energy, because you're going to keep doing what you do and in about 22 years, you're going to be the one writing this letter…

To all the young bulls who read this:

Heed these words that I've said to myself, because if you don't, then like me you'll be looking back on your life from behind a forty-foot wall saying to yourself, "What the Fuck!" If you don't change the things you're doing and the way you're thinking, you'll be writing this same type of letter to yourself….

Wake up, lil homies, Wake up!!!!

Wa Alaikum as Salaam,

Paul J. P.

Letter to My Son

Looking back into my past and I ain't feelin' right.
Close my curtain cause I'm hurtin' in my cell at night.
Broken mirrors keep reflecting how I used to be.
A thousand memories of pain forever follow me.

Reminiscin' bout dah bricks back in my Zulu days.
Messin' wit dem wacks and hammers, I was in my gangsta phase.
Smokin blunts and pullin' stunts when I was seventeen.
Had tah hustle for dah paper wit dah color green.

Son…wherever you may be, I hope you're not like me.
Always love your family and never leave 'em.
Son…I wish that you could know how much I love you, though
I left so long ago and now you're grown.

I've been down since you were four and I was twenty-one.
Never even had the chance to hear you call me Daddy, son.
All these years I've been here, wishing there was some way
I could let you know how much I care.

Never thought about tomorrow, livin' day by day.
Always knew my time was borrowed, knew that I would have to
    pay.
Never thought about or cared if I was right or wrong.
Just hanging on them corners talkin' bout whose money's long.

Son…wherever you may be, I hope you're not like me.
Always love your family and never leave 'em.
Son…I wish that you could know how much I love you, though
I left so long ago and now you're grown.

31

Termaine J. H.

Letter to My Father

Twenty-six years. It's been twenty-six years since I last saw you. Not really you. But the frozen shell of the man you were. Although this is my first letter to you, I always think about you. Wondering what type of man I'd be today had you been here to influence me as only a father could.

I'm thirty-six now. One year older than you were when you passed. I'm officially on uncharted water, blazing a trail for my own son. Yeah, I have a son, Tyhease. You'd be a grandfather ten times over, and a great grand twice. At last count, your twins had nine. Tony—three and Tonya—six, plus one grand.

Ironically, my son was born on May 9th, eight years from the day of your funeral.

It's been hard, Dad. The road's been rough. While I'm proud of the man I've become, I know the roads taken would have been less severe had you been there to remove the dross, correct then re-direct my steps and inform me on what corners not to bend and why, tell me to wait until I can see clearly instead of relying on clairvoyance. I know you would have given me the game on how to spot snakes, even when the grass was high, and not to be deceived by a woman's beauty or the sweetness of her lips until I know for sure her heart belongs to me. I know you would have told me, even then, that I would never know a woman's heart is as deep as the ocean.

I learned all these things and more from experience. Painful experience. Sure, "Experience is the best teacher," but I know on occasion you would have allowed me to fall on my ass just to see what it did to me, how well I responded to failure. I'm also certain you would have been there to pick me up, explain, instill fatherly affection, wisdom from your own experience, encourage then point me in the right direction.

The absence of your presence stunted my growth. Little boys need their fathers. No other man will love them, teach them, encourage them, instill within them the fundamentals of what a man is and does. Certain stepfathers, uncles, big brothers and special men that mothers have in their lives give noble efforts. All moms try. But women can't raise men. Mom put her thing down. I'm sure you were aware of her stiff jabs and fierce attitude. No matter how strong women are, what single mother can really rear-up an obstinate teenage boy without the only man that can dig in his chest and have the boy still love, admire and respect him?

For all boys lacking that fatherly leadership, the allurement and excitement of the streets entices. There's no one to hold them back from walking into the jungle, being raised by wolves. I followed these wolves everywhere they went and did everything they did under the moonlight. I became fascinated with the wild life. The night life. I followed the pack into life-threatening situations, foolish things, landing in juvenile lock-ups. Eventually graduating to the county and then state penitentiary.

A lot of them were killed. A lot of them killed themselves. Some of them became mentally ill. Some are doing life bids in the pen, and some are doing life trapped in their sad lives of contentment, still standing on corners drinking beer, smoking weed, selling drugs and chasing silly women that perpetuate this God-forbidden culture. But God has preserved me. There's no doubt in my mind you've somehow convinced Him not only to protect me, but to be the father I was lacking. When I was doing wrong, I always knew better. That voice of reason was you, Dad.

Even though I've been shot multiple times, I'm in perfectly good health and have a sound mind. Unfortunately I've been incarcerated for over ten years now. How I landed here is a whole 'nother letter. I'll explain in my next one.

Rather than playing catch with you, Dad, I was given a gun by the only fatherly figure I had. The leader of the pack. Instead of you talking to me about the importance of becoming a working man, I became one of the sales persons for coke-cain. And I thought I was right being on the opposite side of the crack pipe. Ignorance. Your absence is no fault of your own. You were taken away prematurely. I never accepted the version of your death told to me as a child. Coincidentally, mom recently told me she only told me the story she was told, that she doesn't accept it either. Only God and those who were there that fateful night with you know.

I don't remember this, but mom said I ran out of the funeral parlor, crying into the middle of the street, nearly hit by a car. I don't remember. At that young age, I was probably running to be with you somehow, someway. Hoping you were outside waiting to take me with you wherever you were going. I do know I kissed your forehead. This is how I know you were frozen. I kissed you good-bye. Because good-bye means forever. And that this would be the last time I touched the one man I can honestly say I loved, knowing I would never see him again. Forever. Does anyone know what that does to the psyche of a child? God, I miss you, Dad. I became envious of all my friends who had their fathers, a foundation to lean upon when the going got tough. Today at thirty-six, I still get jealous of my friends who have their fathers, that bonding relationship. The one person they can always go to for sound wisdom, direction, correction. The older version of themselves. I used to call my older brother and sister's father, "dad." That is how much I needed and wanted a father. Everything I've been doing for the past twenty-six years, I've been doing and learning on my own. And the things I continue to do from this day forward will be on my own. It will all be new to me. When you passed, you had a full head of hair. At thirty-six, my hair is thinning. If I go bald, what would I look like? I recently learned you had seizures. I don't. It's little things like these I wish you were here for.

I can go on and on: I'm certain you'd love that. But I must bring this to an end. I just wanted to let you know what my life has been like without you in it. I promise you this, though. It will not be another twenty-six years before you hear from me again. It will be soon. Know that your family is well. Your children, siblings, nieces, nephews, grand and great grand. We all love and miss you dearly. You'd be proud of the man I've become. The father I am. I am on my way home, and I will raise your grandson the way I know you would have raised me. I will be there for him like I know you wish you were there for me. Rest in peace, Dad. Love always and forever, your eldest son.

P.S. Even though I'm not a junior, as you know, Joseph is my middle name. To a lot of people, I'm known as "Joe." My driving license says Joseph Hicks. You will be with me indefinitely. Love you, Dad.

Paul J. P.

A Mother's Touch

Dear Mommy,

I wish I had an image of you in my mind, but most of my memory of you is just feeling, an emotion. I can't believe it's been nearly five decades since you left. I needed to write this letter to tell you that, in all those years, you never left my heart. I often wish I could travel back in time to when I was that sensitive little boy who loved to fall asleep sitting on your lap while hugging you, with my head resting on the cushion of your breast.

I never blamed you for leaving. No one who witnessed the years of brutal beatings you suffered at Daddy's hands could blame you. Sometimes I wonder if the hate and anger that boiled inside me throughout my youth was more about your leaving than what he did to you. Maybe it was just camouflage to hide the guilt and shame of loving a father who tortured and tormented the person I loved more than anyone or anything in the world. In my mind, your death was not just a suicide; it was also a murder, and Daddy was the killer.

I saw you leap out of your bedroom window that night. I think something important inside me shattered when you crashed through the glass. That window symbolized the best part of my life, broken into a thousand pieces scattered around your twisted body lying on the cold concrete in front of our house on Oriana Street. I didn't know at the time that I would eventually become a predator roaming the streets of that very same neighborhood. Didn't know that Daddy's dark heart would infect me like a contagious disease, that his rage and violence would become mine.

I used to think that my indulgence in alcohol, crime, and gang violence was about nothing more than a youthful thirst for adventure and survival on the streets. I know now that a lot of it was about escaping the pain of an unhappy family life. I needed to find an identity and something to belong to that gave me visibility. Becoming a fierce gang warrior who danced with death seemed to fulfill those needs.

It wasn't until I was condemned to a life sentence in prison for murder that I began to acknowledge some painful truths about myself. In my youth I wore toughness like a black cape to hide a hornet's nest of insecurities stinging my soul. I was hypersensitive to negative criticism, clumsy in sports, and slow in school. I lacked the confidence to be charming and witty around girls I liked because I thought I was too ugly to love. After you died, I felt lost and disconnected from everything.

Most of my pleasant memories of childhood before you died have faded like a picture on a silkscreen tee-shirt that's been washed a thousand times. I don't remember the sound of your voice, the way you walked, or even the touch of your hand. But I never forgot the feeling of being loved whenever you were near. You were my mommy, my somebody to love who loved me. I remember being content just following you around the house all day watching you cook and clean. I remember how the only religious services I enjoyed attending were the family Bible studies at home, when you read stories from the Bible to me, Catherine, Sandy, Roland, and Junior.

In case you didn't already know, Catherine and Sandy never stopped studying the Bible. You would be so proud of them. They both endured a lifetime of hardship and have remained devout Jehovah Witnesses since you passed away. Like me, however, Roland and Junior got caught up in the street life. But they were lucky enough to get out before it was too late and, for the most part, grew up to be hard-working family men. I, on the other hand, got lost in the culture of crime and the criminal justice system swallowed me before I could find my way out.

The huge number of lower-class juvenile delinquents raised in single-parent families headed by women has generated much talk about the importance of a child having a father in his life, especially a male child. As I see it, having a mother is equally important. Just as there are certain things only a man can teach a male child, I believe there are things a boy must learn from a woman in order to fully understand what manhood is all about.

I have no idea how my life would have turned out if you were there to raise me to adulthood. But I do remember enough about you to know that I would have always been able to talk to you about anything I was going through and receive sound advice. During the darkest moments of loneliness and despair, I've prayed to you countless times. I don't know if you heard any of them, but those prayers helped me in many battles with inner demons that threatened my sanity during the course of over 35 years of incarceration.

In reflecting on the level of crime and violence that I had engaged in during my youth, I almost choked on the shame I felt when I realized how I had dishonored your memory by the lifestyle I had embraced. I've devoted many years of my time in prison in pursuit of education that ultimately empowered me to make positive contributions to the lives of others in various forms of community service. I've learned and accomplished things that I never imagined possible when I was a fool running the streets of North Philadelphia. I've met hundreds of highly educated and amazingly caring and compassionate people who actually regard me as their intellectual equal. Some of them have even become valued friends. Transforming into a productive adult after wasting my youth being a destructive menace wasn't easy, but it was well worth the effort.

Sometimes I make myself sad with regret when I think about missed opportunities to do something good with my life in my youth. I wish I had discovered how much more rewarding helping and giving is than hurting and taking before I condemned myself to a life of pain in this spirit-eating beast called prison. Being involved in activities that help others gives my life meaning and purpose and keeps me too busy to waste precious time mourning over the loss of my freedom. However, loneliness still clings to my heart like a leech. I guess, in some ways, I'm still that longing-to-be-hugged child who misses his mother's touch.

Love,
Paul

Suggestions for Writing

1. Read James T.'s letter to his younger self. How does the letter make you feel about education. Next, read Paul P.'s "Literacy and Sour Grapes" in the Decisions section. How does this piece's message compare to James's message in his letter? Now, write yourself a letter about your own educational experience. What are your hopes in terms of your education?

2. Write a letter to yourself discussing a moment when you made a decision that you wish you could take back.

3. Write a letter to yourself in the future or past.

4. Read D. Saadiq P.'s letter. Did you ever do something for a friend, even though you knew it was wrong? If yes, how do you feel now about that decision? If no, how do you feel about D. Saadiq's actions? What could he have done differently?

5. Read Paul P.'s letter to his son. What is one thing that you've done or are doing that you would never want your son or daughter to do? Or, what is one thing you can start changing about yourself that will give you a better chance for a happy future?

6. Read Charles D.'s letter to his younger self. Do you believe that you can create your own destiny? Why or why not? Can you visualize your future?

DECISIONS

Paul J. P.

A Dark Heart's Whisper

I grew up in Philadelphia in the nineteen sixties and seventies. My family lived in neighborhoods where practically every day was characterized by a series of potentially deadly street encounters. Gang violence that extended back several generations before I was born placed virtually every youth in the community at risk of being robbed, beaten, or killed each time they walked outside of their home. Like thousands of other kids, I became a product of the street gang culture I was raised in, adopting an attitude and value system that I believed was imperative for my survival and sense of identity. By age 17, it was obvious even to me that my self-proclaimed ghetto fame as a gangsta would end in an early death or life in prison. Still, there was always the soft whisper from deep inside that said, "You are more."

I was in my mid teens when I gave serious pause to think about the consequences of the lifestyle I had chosen in my youth. It happened following a street gang incident where I had come to the rescue of a younger member of my gang. I can almost visualize the entire incident as if it happened yesterday.

On our way to the liquor store to cop a half gallon of Thunder Bird wine, four of my homies and I ran into one of my young-bucks (a younger gang member); three dudes from another gang had him hemmed up on the corner. Fidgeting like a horse ready to break out the gates on a racetrack, he was clearly intimidated by these guys. It was just starting to get dark and they apparently hadn't noticed us walking up on them. As we got closer, I recognized this one guy from a gang whose territory bordered ours.

We had almost reached the corner when I yelled out to my young-buck in the most serious tone I could muster, "Yo, Zoom, what up?" Spontaneously jerking his head in our direction, he recognized us and responded with a glimmer of relief in his eyes. I broke right through the semicircle they had formed around him, stepped to Zoom and said, "You a'ight gang?" Then I turned to the guy I recognized from the other gang, looked him dead in the eyes and said, "What's all this about, Wolf?"

Only 16 at the time, I had very few negotiating or mediating skills. I only knew the rules of the game. Hesitate, flinch, or communicate fear and you could easily become the plaything of a vicious street predator. About my age, Wolf was warlord of the midgets (gang members between ages 12 and 16). His two young-bucks looked like they were around Zoom's age, 13 or 14. Obviously fucked up on wine or something, they stared at me with piercing eyes and faces twisted like someone had just passed gas while I was talking to Wolf.

It turns out that they were after Zoom because, according to Wolf, he was supposed to be from their corner (one of several terms we used that simply means gang—e.g., crew, way, or corner). They were accusing him of being a corner hopper and wanted to take him back to their turf and give him the line (beat him up) for not coming down the way.

"Yall ain't taking him no where," I told them. "If he really is from your way and wants to get out, he can give out fair-ones (fist fights) right here and now."

I had personally drafted Zoom into our gang almost a year earlier and wasn't about to let them come and just take somebody from my crew.

Looking at Zoom like he was a piece of shit, Wolf said, "You wanna get out the gang, pussy? Then you gotta fight me first."

With his pants legs shaking like he had a mini-fan in his pocket, Zoom hunched his shoulders while cocking his head to the side and curled his lips in tight. Then he took off his Coolcap, stuffed it in his back pocket, and said, "Let's do this."

They stepped into the street to rumble. That's when one of Wolf's young-bucks got in my face and said, "Who the fuck are you!" I mugged him in the face with the palm of my hand so hard that he fell on his ass. He jumped up and the other young-buck joined him in a halfhearted attempt to rush me. Meanwhile, Zoom panicked and demonstrated how he earned his nickname with an amazing 747 move. "Get back here, you bitch-ass mothafucka," I yelled. But he was "gone with the wind."

After Zoom ran, I got into it with Wolf. While we were fighting, his two young-bucks found two pieces of dirty, old, splinter-filled two-by-fours, and I found myself in the middle of the street trying to fight off all three of them. When I noticed my homies hadn't moved a muscle to help me, I thought to myself, "Dem pussies just gon' stand there and not do shit!" From that point on everything happened in a flash. I slipped my hand in my pocket to grab my knife. One of Wolf's young-bucks had maneuvered his way behind me and was a blink away from bashing me in the back of the head when my homie, Dukes, intervened and snatched the stick from him.

In the next instant, I somehow tripped and was falling on top of Wolf as the sound of a car horn and screeching brakes invaded my ears. The car had come to a full stop only inches from hitting both of us. I rolled off Wolf, sprang to my feet and noticed there was no blade in my knife, just the handle in my hand. The blade had broken off in Wolf's neck. I took off running down the street and stopped after about a quarter of a block and turned around. To my surprise, Wolf and his homies were running in the other direction back towards their turf.

Back on the corner, I gave Dukes props for getting my back and we headed for the liquor store. I said nothing to my two other young-bucks about their cowardly inaction. Like Zoom, they were new recruits with little gang war experience and had become paralyzed with fear. All of my hostility was directed towards Zoom because his running out made me and my crew look bad.

* * * *

Back from the liquor store with the wine, there were now about eight of us—including my younger brother, Roland. We were hanging out on the steps of an abandoned house in the middle of the block, across the street from my homie Mike's house. I lived down the street a ways with my father, younger sister, and two younger brothers. It was a small street about two blocks from where the incident with Wolf and his homies jumped off.

Lost in the haze of the wine and metal cleaning solvent we were sniffing that we called "Tyawa," I had forgotten all about the earlier incident with Wolf. Then I learned what is meant by the saying, "All hell broke loose." Without warning, a swarm of guys from Wolf's gang turned the corner and came charging at us with bad intentions. Mike and several of my other homies ran across the street into Mike's house. My brother Roland, Dukes, and me took off in the opposite direction, with Wolf's homies right on our ass. We ran right past my house because I didn't want them to know where I lived; plus, if the door was locked we might not have had time to unlock it. The other end of the block was cut off from Montgomery Avenue by an old hat factory, so we had to turn on another small street to get to the larger street the next block over, 3rd Street.

When we hit 3rd Street, I saw my youngest brother, Junior, sitting on the steps with some of his friends who lived in the house on the corner right where the small street came out into 3rd. As soon as they saw us running with the guys from the other gang dead on our shit, Junior and his friends ran in the house and slammed the door.

I had no idea of how much damage I had done to Wolf when I stabbed him. But it was apparently bad enough for his gang to mobilize and invade our turf in full force. I can't say for sure if they were forty, fifty, or a hundred strong. All I know is that they were coming from everywhere. When we came out of the small street from my block, there were more of them coming down 3rd from Berks. With a bunch of guys behind us and more coming from Berks Street, we cut across 3rd Street and ran up another small street, intending to double back towards Columbia Avenue.

We put a little distance between them, but Roland couldn't keep up with us and started falling behind. In an attempt to lose our pursuers, we cut through an abandoned lot full of bricks, broken bottles and weeds. The maneuver seemed to have worked, but my brother had disappeared in the process. There was nothing we could do except keep running and hope he just decided to break off and duck into an abandoned house or something.

Believing we had lost Wolf's gang by cutting through that lot and running down another small street, I was beginning to feel a sense of relief. But as soon as we stepped on Columbia Avenue, we were spotted and took off running again headed towards 2nd Street. By this time we were completely exhausted and just slowed to a staggering walk with God knows how many guys still running in full stride behind us and rapidly closing the gap.

As we were walking towards 2nd Street, gasping to catch our breath while Wolf's gang closed in for the kill, I realized that running in this direction was a bad move. We had been forced to run in an area where there were very few streetlights and no houses or people to witness the nightmare we would live, or die from, if we got caught. Surrounded by huge old factory buildings that slept through the night, we had stumbled into the perfect place to get stomped and stabbed undisturbed.

With my lungs still on fire from lack of oxygen, I flagged Dukes yelling, "Come on, man," and took off running again. Running like a drunk man, he was about to run straight across 2nd Street until I yelled, "Not that way, man!" Dukes was originally from across town and didn't know our neighborhood that well. He didn't know that he was about to run right into the white boys' neighborhood. Going anywhere across 2nd Street at night was like crashing a Ku Klux Klan rally.

We ran a little ways down 2nd Street towards Montgomery Avenue and cut through an empty lot leading to a train depot that sometimes held up to 60 boxcars. Dukes and I ran across the train tracks scurrying like rodents through the maze of boxcars until we were deep inside the depot. Only seconds after we disappeared among the boxcars, we heard someone not far behind us shout, "They ran this way!" In a hushed tone I said, "Come on, Dukes," and crawled through dirt and gravel to get underneath one of the boxcars. Dukes followed without hesitation and we lay still trying desperately to suppress our heavy breathing, fearing it might give us away.

No sooner than we crawled under the train, the sound of running feet crunching gravel found our ears. Guys were shouting things like, "Where dah fuck dey at?" "You see em, Lefty?" "Damn!" "Dey was just right here!" We could see various sized dress shoes and Chuck Taylor sneaks darting by attached to the bottom half of khakis and dress slacks.

Then just like that, we were alone in the silence of the night.

As we lay waiting to make sure they were gone, I suddenly realized that I was still clutching the soda bottle containing the Tyawah we had been sniffing when Wolf's gang started chasing us. Knowing how that stuff can feel like burning acid when exposed to the skin, I had planned to smash the first guy that grabbed me in the face with the soda bottle if we got caught. Now out of immediate danger, my thoughts drifted backwards, replaying the events that carried us to this point. Then, like stepping barefoot on the third rail of a subway track, a terrible surge of fear suddenly shot through my body. My stomach felt like it had turned inside out. Sure, I was afraid when we were being chased because we were literally running for our lives. But that was a fear that I was intimately familiar with from being chased and shot at on numerous occasions since I was 12 years old. It was a fear that I had come to perversely perceive as sort of a rush, part of the thrill of the game.

This other fear was different, something indescribably painful I had never felt before and never wanted to feel again. It hit me when I thought about my brother, Roland. *Did I get my brother killed*, I thought to myself. *Is he lying somewhere leaking blood on the sidewalk or in a dark empty lot, beaten to a pulp, stabbed or filleted like a piece of sushi?* The next thoughts immediately following those were even scarier, *Did I run out on my own brother? Why didn't I go back for him when he disappeared in that lot on Bodine Street?*

Overwhelmed with feelings of guilt and shame, I began arguing with myself, *Naw, fuck dat! There wasn't shit you could do because there were too many of them.*

But you big Snake from Zulu Nation, mothafucka, I told myself. *You dah nigga who fought a grown ass Puerto Rican barehanded when he was comin' at you with a shank, the nigga dat chased 15 of dem Diamond Street pussies by yourself and ran from a cop who pulled his gun out and had you jammed up at pointblank range. How could you get all bent out of shape because Zoom ran out on you and then turn right around and run out on your own fuckin' brotha?*

It didn't take long for me to convince myself that the situation with my brother wasn't the same as what Zoom did. He ran because he was scared to fight one dude. What I did was a rational, strategic decision based on the reasonable assumption that my brother just decided to cut away from Dukes and me to hide somewhere because he couldn't run fast enough to keep up. But the thought that I ran out on my brother and had gotten him killed lingered in my mind as Dukes and I crawled from under the boxcar to go looking for him.

We ran back to the lot where he disappeared but couldn't find him. Next, we went to Foot's house on 3rd street, where my baby brother, Junior, had run. Junior and his friends were all right, but Roland wasn't there either. Finally, we went to Mike's house, where he and my other homies had run when Wolf's gang first started chasing us. I was in Mike's house going off. "Y'all see Roland," I shouted. With eyes glazed full of unspilled tears, I shouted again, "I gotta find my fuckin' brotha!"

I headed outside with the rest of my homies following. As soon as we stepped outside, here comes Roland bouncing down the street with a stupid-looking grin on his face. "Nigga, where dah fuck you been?" I said, trying to play it off like his showing up was no big deal. He said, "Man, I couldn't keep up with you and Dukes. I broke off and ducked into those weeds in the lot and just stayed there until I was good and sure dem niggaz was long gone." Dukes cut in and said, "Dam, shorty, we been lookin' everywhere for yo dumb ass. You a'ight?"

Forty years would lapse before I found out what really happened when Roland ducked into those weeds that night. He came to visit me at Graterford prison in 2011, and I told him I was writing the story about what happened that night. I was blown away when he told me that after he had cut away from me and Dukes, a guy from the gang that was chasing us found him trying to hide inside the weeds in the empty lot he had run into. He said the guy had a shotgun and looked him square in the face but didn't say a word. The guy just shot a blast from the shotgun into the weeds right next to where he was crouched and shouted to his homies, "There's nobody here," and then ran away.

* * * *

I'm filled with shame whenever I think about how my brother

49

could have been killed that day because of the lifestyle I was living. The internal whisper telling me that I was more than just a street thug didn't really have much of an impact on me even after that incident. But it eventually became a life transforming shout. Sadly, though, that didn't happen until my indulgence in gang violence earned me a life sentence without the possibility of parole for the murder of a rival gang member in 1976. I was 19 at the time and have been incarcerated for that crime since 1977.

D. Saadiq P.

DÉJÀ VU

Imagine waking up in a strange metal bed in an unfamiliar room with a dim light on in the middle of the wall. You rise up and wonder, *Where am I?* The walls are drab off-white. Everything is plain. You get out of the bed and walk to the large door with the rectangular window; your mind races, thinking all kinds of crazy things. Am I in a hospital, a mental institution? Did somebody kidnap me, or worst of all, am I dead?

You look out the window to see more doors, but not a hallway of doors. They're in some sort of circle or octagonal shape, and the room is big. The lights are very bright, and the white walls and brown doors with rectangular windows are like the ones you're looking through. As your brain absorbs what is happening, you start to notice people walking around, all dressed in the same dark blue pants and shirts, but they aren't going anywhere. They are just walking around aimlessly in circles.

You try to focus on the faces to see if you recognize any of them, but they are all blurry, like your eyes can only focus on your surroundings and every time you attempt to look at these mysterious faces, your vision becomes blurred again.

Now you're really tripping. Am I in the twilight zone? What should I do? Should I go out there? Should I stay in here? As your mind starts to contemplate what to do next, the door suddenly opens and you step out into this weird-looking place that you've never been to before; as you turn to walk in the direction of the people in blue, you notice a large mirror out of the corner of your eye. You turn, and there you are, dressed in the same dark blue clothing. Your face is clear; you can see yourself. It's you. When you turn to look at the others' faces again, they are blurry!

You say out loud, "What the fuck is going on? Where am I?!!"

The people in blue stop and look at you, but they don't say anything.

You look around the room and now you notice some funny-looking chairs or couches, and two TVs suspended on the wall. You look at the TVs, but you are still unable to make anything out as you walk closer to them. Nothing is making any sense. You become tired and confused, so you decide to sit down on the funny-looking couches made of some hard plastic material. As you sit there trying to understand where you are and what the hell is going on, one of the doors opens up and a tall figure in blue comes out with a big white bag slung over his shoulder. He waves at you and proceeds to walk across the big room to another door unlike any of the others. You just noticed it was there, and he walks out.

As soon as the tall figure makes his exit through the steel-colored door, three people dressed in blue get up from the couches and run towards the door that the tall dude with the bag just exited. They go in and moments later they come out with stuff that you can't make out in their hands, and go in different directions towards separate brown doors, disappearing behind them.

Upon seeing this, you jump up and run to the door they just came out of and look in. You see nothing. It looks like the same room you came out of, so you run to the next one, and again the same thing. You look for the steel door, but now it is gone. You run around the room looking for the steel door, but there isn't one. You search and search, until you finally give up and walk back to the door you came out of and go back in. It slams. Bam!

You wake!

This is a dream that I had when I was around 16 or 17 years old, and ever since I was little my grandmother used to tell me to always remember my dreams and tell her about them so she could look them up and play her numbers with the number that the dream represents in her dream book. This is some down south shit old people used to play the numbers with, and if my grandmother hit, she would give me half of what she won, so I was always calling her up and telling her about my dreams. Even now I do, but there was something about this particular dream; she couldn't find a number for it, and she couldn't figure it out. She made me repeat it 4 or 5 times and still came up with nothing, so finally she concluded, it must be a sign or something, and left it like that.

I never forgot about the dream, and I would tell people about it from time to time to see if they knew what it meant, but each time I was unsuccessful.

So fast-forward a couple of years, and I am on the run hiding out in Florida when I got locked up on an unrelated case.

Now, I've been locked up before as a juvenile, but never as an adult, so county jail was going to be a new experience for me in itself. But being 1800 miles away from home and locked up would be a whole different situation.

So after about two days on the block, I'm sitting down on this hard bluish grey two-man couch watching TV with some dudes that I knew from Tallahassee. The Block Officer sitting at the console calls out a cell number and this dark-skinned dude from Jacksonville gets up from one of the other couches on the other side of the block and walks to the console. The C/O tells him that "Your papers come in. Go pack your shit cause you're out of here!"

Jacksonville smiled and ran to his cell and about five minutes later he came out with a "Big White Laundry Bag" full of his stuff and threw up two fingers and said, "I'm out, folk. I hope to see y'all on the other side!" He walked to the sally port and was gone, and after a few seconds had passed, three dudes who were also from Jacksonville got up and went into his cell. Minutes later they came out with what he left behind, and they took the leftovers to their cells.

I was sitting there watching the whole thing take place in total disbelief, because this was the crazy ass dream that I had dreamt years ago. I didn't know what it meant then, but I do now. I turned to my man named Derrick from Tallahassee and said, "Yo, this is some Déjà Vu Shit!" and I told him about the dream.

After telling Derrick about the dream, I called my Grandmother and told her what happened, and she said, "I told you it was a sign, but damn, I didn't think it would be this bad."

I hung up after a few minutes and looked around to take everything in and it all fit. The white walls, the brown doors with the rectangular window, the plastic couches, everything with the exception of the steps to the top tier, the phones, the yard, the console, the C/O and the now-clear faces.

I shook my head and went to my cell, and when the door closed, Bam! I looked around the cell. Ironically I didn't really pay any attention to the cell when I first got there two days before, but there was the metal bunk bed, the drab off-white walls and the dim light.

As I took it all in, I said to myself, turning to look out the door, *If only I knew.*

Fifteen years later, *I am still waiting to wake up!*

Mwandishi M.

THE LOST BOY

Philadelphia, Pennsylvania 1988

The loud subway train boomed through the tunnel at a fast speed.

"Next stop, Ellsworth & Federal," said the SEPTA orange-line subway conductor over the P.A. system. SEPTA is an acronym for the public transportation system in Philly. It stands for: Southeastern Pennsylvania Transit Authority.

"Like we don't know where tha fuck we're going!" I said loud enough for anyone in earshot. I was a smart-aleck fifteen-year-old kid who thought he knew everything.

An old white woman wearing a terrible-looking wig sitting across from me clutched her purse to her bosom. That gesture always infuriated me. I was a young African-American male and hated when women of any color felt threatened by me as if I were some type of savage.

The train slowed down as it pulled into Ellsworth-Federal station. When the train stopped and the doors opened I said to the old woman, "Bitch! Don't nobody want chur fuckin' purse!" then walked onto the platform. I banged on the window startling her as the train resumed its route. Blue sparks shot up from the third rail as the train disappeared into a black tunnel of nothingness.

As I ascended the steps, the foul smell of urine reached my nose. Trash was strewn all over the walkway. I followed behind the other patrons exiting the subway seemingly without a care in the world. Coming home from school was always better than going! Most of the time I hopped the turnstile or squeezed through a bent exit turnstile because I'd sold my school tokens. I laughed at the history lesson in school that day about forty acres and a mule. What the hell did I need with a mule? I had an iron horse!

My house was a two-minute walk from Broad & Ellsworth. I lived on the dead-end block of Carlisle Street behind St. Rita's Catholic

Basilica. I stayed with my Gram, Pop-Pop, and cousin, Tyke.

God bless Gram. She worked so hard! She was up by 3:00 a.m. preparing coffee for herself and my older female cousin, Peanut. Gram had to be at work by 5:00 a.m. at a garment factory on 4th & Girard Avenue. Usually, she'd beat me home.

When I came through the front door there was Pop-Pop who was called "Horse" by all those who knew him. He'd be in his usual seat right in front of the television.

"Hey Pop," I said.

He gave me a blank stare and didn't say anything. I swear he hated me, but for the life of me I couldn't figure out why. Maybe because all the shit I thought I got away with, he knew I did. Mainly because he'd done it himself when he was my age.

Gram was in the kitchen preparing dinner. As I look back on it, damn, did she ever get any rest? To come home from work, just to go to work cooking for us! What a strong woman she was.

I shot upstairs, threw my books on my bed, and grabbed my switchblade, rolling papers, Sony Walkman and Public Enemy cassette tape. My homies and I sometimes had beef with other neighborhoods so I had to make sure I had my knife with me. Then I ran down the steps, heading for the front door.

"C'mere, Dishi!" Her voice halted me in my tracks, making me do an immediate about-face and head into the kitchen.

Gram's name was Elizabeth, and she was a beautiful red-bone with silky hair. Her hazel eyes could stop a Brink's truck. In her late fifties, she didn't look a day over forty. She wore furry slippers and a flower-print housecoat.

"Where you runnin' off to so fast?"

"Peters Street, Gram. You know dat'z where I be."

"Anngh unngh, whut about chur homework?"

"Ain't got none. We got oral homework," I said, lying through my teeth.

"Why do you keep hanging wit' 'dem boyz down on Peters Street?"

Why do pigs love slop? I said internally. "Gram, dey my friendz down there."

56

"You're headed for trouble. I'm not coming to bail you outta jail. Jus' so you know," she said while cutting greens on the cutting board.

"I'm not doin' nuffin', dough."

"Alright. You heard whut I said. C'mon in here at eight so you can eat. Put my pots away when you finish, too."

As always, what she said went in one ear and directly out the other. Shit, by 7:00 that evening Gram would be asleep, dead to the world on the couch to get her rest so she could be ready for work the next morning. I could come in at 11:00 and she wouldn't know!

When I got outside I pushed the "play" button on my Walkman, as Chuck D's bellowing voice sent chills through me:

I got a letter from tha government tha otha' day,
I opened, and read it, it said dey wuz suckaz!
Dey wanted me fo' tha Army or whuteva',
Picture me givin' a damn, I said neva'!

A young revolutionary in training is what I was. Fuck the establishment, fuck the status quo, and most definitely, fuck the police! I had a right to be hostile; my people were being persecuted.

By the time I got to the middle of Ellsworth Street, before 13th, the smell of Pete's Pizzeria made my stomach growl. The smell of fried onions and grilled steak coming from the exhaust fan was unmistakable. South Philly is the cheesesteak capital of the world! I peeped in but none of my crew was in there. Pete's was one of our hangout spots. They had a "Double-Dragon" video game machine in there. At least five hundred quarters of mine went into that machine.

A minute later I hit my destination at 12th & Ellsworth, making a left walking towards Peters Street. The whole crew was on the corner of 12th & Peters. All my homies: Jay-Tee was the oldest and basically the leader. His funny-shaped feet made his sneakers lean to the side. Rome was second in command. He had a crazy girlfriend across the bridge in Camden, New Jersey. Ace was the comedian; he had jokes for days and could always make the best out of a bad situation. Rommel was the enforcer—250 lbs of heaviness, "Re-Run" incarnate! Terrence was the handball champ. He thought he was John McEnroe. Gerald was the first to get his driver's license and have a car to drive us around.

Edison, the quiet one - silent but deadly! Tyke, my cousin, was a year younger than me. He was the hoop star. The first one of us all to get a full scholarship to a university for his basketball skills. The Pee-wees: Jamel, Jay-Tee's little brother. Kareem, Gerald's little brother. My three little cousins, Raheem, Minute, and Devon. Raheem had more hustle in him than all of us. He started running errands for "Skinny" Joey Merlino when Joey owned the café shop on 12th & Annin Streets (but that's another story). Lastly, "Fat" Kenny and his little brother Quadir, A.K.A. Dupot. They had moved into our neighborhood from North Philly, and they were more street-smart than us all.

They were all huddled around Dupot. From what I could see he had a new coat on. A butterscotch three-quarter shearling! A coat that in '88 cost every bit of $800. All eyes were fixed on Dupot.

"Damn, dat jawn iz phat Dupot. When did ju get dat?" I asked, as my hands were now feeling on the butter-soft leather.

"Yesterday, dope ain't it?" he asked smiling. His gold cap on his front crown tooth shone in the sunlight.

One of the old-head crack addicts, Spoody, came past us. He headed towards the projects on 13th & Catharine, notoriously known as "Saigon." We all knew he was headed to the projects to get his drugs.

"Yo, Spoody, I got sum' shit right here," Dupot said, pulling out a plastic bag filled with caps that had red tops.

My eyes widened in excitement. It wasn't the first time I saw caps before, not by any means. But it was the first time anyone in our crew had drugs for sale.

Spoody looked at the bag filled with caps. "Lemme get three for fourteen," Spoody said as he pulled the crumpled Hamilton and four singles from his pocket.

"Yeah, you can get dat," replied Dupot matter-of-factly.

Out of us all, Dupot had the best clothes and material possessions. The first one to have Gucci sneakers and a thick herringbone chain. I wanted the things he had because those material possessions brought admiration, respect, power, and most of all, girls!

"Dishi, you got papers?" Jay-Tee asked.

"You know it!" I replied.

Only the oldest of us smoked, took pills and drank cough syrup. We sat on the corner steps smoking weed and drinking 40-oz bottles of Coqui 900. My mind was focused on getting crack to sell. I wanted to come up. Later on that evening I pulled Dupot to the side so that I could get in his ear about letting me hustle. He told me he was going to see his connection in a few days and he'd let me know. A few days was too long to wait. I wanted money and prestige now!

Three days later I met Dupot on the corner of 12th & Peters Street. The block was a dead end and Spoody lived in the last house. It was dilapidated and needed many repairs. But it was a place where we could go to cap up our drugs.

Dupot had a pretty good connection from his old neighborhood in North Philly. The connection was a member of the "Junior Black Mafia" gang, which wreaked havoc on the streets of Philadelphia in the late 80s to early 90s.

We went into Spoody's house and the smell of his living room was putrid! The kitchen was in the back and that's where Dupot and I sat at the kitchen table. Dupot pulled a big plastic bag filled with crack cocaine from his coat pocket along with an eight-ounce pharmacy bottle of cough syrup. From his jeans pocket he pulled out a couple bags of empty caps with yellow tops.

"A, Spoody, where'z dat scale I brought ova' here yesterday?" Dupot asked as I waited to see what this experience was going to be like.

"Unda' tha sink. Whut chu got fo' me, dough?" he asked with his crack pipe in his hand. With his free hand he scratched his arms.

"Hold on a second, damn. Lemme weight this shit first," Dupot answered.

The hard crack looked like frozen cookie dough. Dupot sat the triple-beam scale on the table and weighed the crack. It amounted to 28 grams, which is an ounce. He weighed out seven grams and set it to the side. Then he got a razor blade and a mirror that he set the seven grams on. Dupot broke off a small piece and handed it to Spoody.

Spoody's hand shook as he put a smaller piece of crack onto the top of the glass stem that contained burned Brillo, which served as a screen. Spoody picked up the matchbook and removed two matches together.

With the crack pipe in his left hand and the matches in the right, he struck the matches using the striker that was on the matchbook. Once the matches were lit, he held the stem at a 45° angle, making contact with the crack that was loaded at the top of the stem. A crackling sound could be heard as gray smoke filled the stem as he inhaled the potent smoke, holding it in for as long as he could. A huge cloud of smoke exited his mouth once he exhaled.

It was clear that the feeling of euphoria once again took ahold of his body as he relished the effects of the crack working in his system. The crack released thousands of neurotransmitters called dopamine. However, the feeling was short lived, as four to five minutes later the effects wore off. He threw another piece of crack on the stem and repeated the process.

"A'ight, shave it down like this Dishi," Dupot said while the razor blade moved back and forth shaving the once hard crack into powder.

I was a little nervous. I removed the top from the pharmacy bottle and took a nice pop of the purple Promethazine VC. It immediately soothed my nerves as it went down my throat. I started shaving the crack down with the razor blade exactly as I was instructed to by Dupot.

We had "illusion" caps that were plastic and I don't know how they did it, but it magnified the contents inside of the caps making it seem as if more crack was in it than it really contained. At the top of the capsule was a line to let you know how much crack to put in so you would have enough room to put the top on.

That day was the beginning of my hustling career. The day the lost boy became really, really lost.

I want to appear in front of that dumb stupid kid capping up crack like a Charles Dickens classic, an apparition, "The Ghost of Future Lost!" Try and talk some sense into him before it's too late. Tell him to finish school and pursue a college education. I want to tell him not to be so caught up in the hatred of the forefathers like Washington, Jefferson, Madison and the rest, slave owners who considered him three-fourths of a man when they wrote the Constitution. The men whose faces were on the very currency he was trying to acquire.

That kid needs to know knowledge is power and can empower

him to be anything he wants to be in life. Knowledge doesn't dissipate. It always wants to be retained and used. Knowledge also understands that it has an enemy. An enemy that would seek out and destroy it like an HIV cell.

Would he even heed my warning? What if I told him that in a few years Dupot would be dead, shot in the head from a self-inflicted coup de grace! Or believe that Gram was telling him the truth when she told him he was headed for trouble? But knowing him, he would ignore the warning from his older, wiser self. You could tell that kid not to touch the stove because it was hot, but he'd touch it anyway just for confirmation. Stupid kid, he wouldn't let his brain develop into effulgence!

When I wrote this piece I wanted to give the reader some idea of what it was like for me growing up on the impoverished streets of urban South Philadelphia. I pray I painted a clear and convincing portrait. But it's hard to get every little detail when you're painting with a broad brush. For the most part, the memory is true and concise.

As a young teenager it was easy for me to be blinded by money and material possessions. The man speaking to you today knows the hypocrisy of that lifestyle. The man speaking to you today believes the continuous circle of selling drugs and killing his own people for profit is detestable! If I had to do it all again, like Frost, I would have taken the road less traveled.

Through my hardships I have become a better man. I've learned so much over the years. Change is an evolutionary process that continues day by day. But once again, I would've told the younger me this profound parable: Search for a beautiful heart and not beautiful things. Beautiful things aren't always good, but good things are always beautiful.

Christopher R. W. M.

HERE AM I

I am told that in order to heal, I must first
forgive those of my past. How can I excuse the
bloody butchery that you inflicted upon me? The
ignorance of bigotry wrenched from me like a
dollar bill taken by a bully.

I often live in the splattered blood that you
spilled in 1989—I can't seem to let go of the
memories—they stick to me like a tattoo—
always there to try to remind me that I'm one-
third of a human being.

You called me a nigger as you mauled my head with
your wooden pipes—my screams were stifled by
swollen lips that busted open with reddened pus.

Yet, to move on, I must first pardon you. If
not, restoration will evade me like a frightened
baby hare running from a hungry wolf. To
upgrade, I must broaden my intellect to move
beyond nineteen eighty nine, and dwell on two
thousand and eleven.

Yet memory chains me to two decades of
horrible images—the screams of tortured souls
still wake me in the wee hours of the night—I
embraced your forename "nigger," and your
abusiveness towards me, as you treated me like
a dog that defecated on your kitchen floor.

A swift kick in the stomach, a club to the head,
quieted me so long ago. Your hot brand on my arm

reminds me not of the searing pain, but
that I must finally move beyond your hate-filled
reddened faces and tobacco-filled mouths.

To heal today, I **must** forgive and forget. If I
don't, then I am no better than you, and the acts
that you perpetrated on me so long ago.

Yes, I'm finally ready to forgive you. At last,
I'm willing to embrace freedom—liberated from
my past recollections, my present mental
internments, and my uncertain future. Freedom
calls, and I'm answering, "Here Am I."

Eduardo R.

WELCOME TO HELL

There was a time when I didn't know what culture shock was. I wouldn't have been able to explain it even if I had been possessed by the ghost of Noah Webster. It's not that I was unfamiliar with different cultures; I was born to Puerto Rican parents who were fairly traditional—as far as Latino traditions go—in their approach to family life. I was raised in a predominantly Black neighborhood, and I attended schools with mostly white students. Sure, the differences were there: language, background, point of view—all influenced by their respective cultures. But the most important similarity, for me at least, was the idea that we were all rooted in the American working-class experience; an experience that was marked mostly by modest homes built on the wages of forty-hour work weeks, social circles that pitched in to improve our neighborly way of living, and a common dream of health and happiness.

It's not like life was ever perfect. The grind was always real, always present. I remember the grease-filled factories and the tiresome ride home in exhaust-fumed buses; the huddled masses in cramped seats, nodding off after a long day, heads swaying gently as the bus chugged along the boulevard and past the vacant lots that used to be residential housing. The city planners had figured that urban blight and its sin of broken windows had cut too deep; gentrification was ushered in to heal the wound: first, by buying homes under market value, then by razing entire city blocks and making way for upscale housing, strip malls, cafes, bistros and boutiques—none of which were locally owned. Long-time residents could no longer afford the increasing property taxes, and so mass-migration set in motion. There were town hall meetings; community members protested in earnest, but when the big money rolls in so too do the bulldozers and wrecking balls. But amid the physical change of row homes that stood for decades was the familial spirit of community living that had always touched my life. Nothing could have prepared me for the world-change from my nine-to-five public life to the twenty-four/seven lockdown of prison.

It was the first time I'd seen a prison wall. The county jail that held me for almost two years resembled the factories that I was used to: linoleum-tiled floors that were buffed and waxed regularly and pneumatic doors with Plexiglas windows. The make-up of the county lock-up had me thinking that the prisons of old were just boogeyman stories that aging, toothless jailbirds used to scare straight the hardheaded kids who thought they were too hip to ever end up in a cage.

Hillside was different. The weathered, brown stones looked as if they'd been cut from ancient caves and stacked by the hands of Vikings; granite walls, checked every hundred-feet or so by turrets and manned by expressionless robots with long-barreled shotguns, rose into the sky and blocked out the sun with imposing authority. The iron gate groaned as it lifted, echoing in my ears like a ghostly howl, and gave us entrance into the mouth of a dungeon.

I was part of a group made up mostly of young men barely out of high school. We were hairless and firm, not yet broken by the long road of time, and too egotistical to realize that prison is used as an organized tool to change one's way of thinking. Some change for better, some for worse.

Welcome to hell! The ruddy-faced lieutenant said. Wild-eyed and tight-lipped, his jaw muscles clenched, making golf ball-sized knots right below his ears. He was short, but powerfully built like a pitbull, and he stalked before us in slow, even, and methodical steps. We stood in a row, naked, except for the haphazardly folded uniform that we held over our privates to protect some idea of modesty, while he delivered his orientation.

This is Hillside. This is the place where all other prisons send their trash, because this is the place where rules are learned. You will all learn the rules or suffer the penalties...

AND I DO MEAN *SUFFER!* In fact, you should expect to suffer. You should expect to suffer even if you manage to follow the rules. For those of you looking to make parole your first time up, you will be sorely disappointed; and for those of you with life, this is the place where you will die.

The squeaking of his highly polished boots could be heard as he turned to leave us on that ominous note. With trembling hands we dressed and picked up what belongings we had.

A make-shift processing station had been set up: a folding table, the boards of which time had warped and left chipped at the edges, and an old, schoolroom chair—straight-backed, that creaked under pressure—was positioned at the end of the long tier. The late-summer wind swirled and carried the stale scent of sweat and cheap tobacco smoke, and the high-pitched crackle of radios bounced off the drab, eggshell-white painted brick walls. We marched along in our wrinkled brown trousers and shirt to the whisper of older cons whose taunts served as entertainment in what was otherwise a laughless place. The processing of men into the hopeless halls of Hillside—which had the dubious honor of being nicknamed *Killside*—was more for show than an actual procedure to track men into appropriate programs. Smokers were housed with non-smokers, security levels were mixed without regard to safety, everyone was enrolled in school—or in what served as an education department—and even guys who had been sober as a saint were scheduled for substance abuse therapy. Bodies were all that counted, statistics to keep State and Federal funding coming in to pay the bills.

The grayness of the housing unit seemed to clash with the floral-printed scrubs worn by the nurse furiously scribbling notes into a medical file. The more I watched her the closer I came to realizing that Hillside was a stone and iron virus that infected the mind. Maybe it was the old lead-based paint, or asbestos in the lungs. Whatever the case, she interrogated the new-commits with a razor-like sharpness. She closed one folder and waved me over. As I sat in the wobbly, wooden chair, unnerved and uncomfortable from the shock of it all, I listened as she spoke without directly looking at me:

Institutional number? she asked with a quality that was more cyborg than human.

DN6284, I said, uncertain if I was correct.

She kept her chin tucked downward and spoke in a clipped monotone: I'm gonna list your family, medical, and mental health history. This will go by quicker if you only interrupt me if anything is incorrect. Got it?

Before I could say a word she proceeded to rattle off my life story:

NAME/Edward Ramirez
AGE/21
HEIGHT/5' 8"
WEIGHT/180 pounds
EYES/Brown
HAIR/Brown
MOTHER/Marissa Ramirez
FATHER/Edwin Ramirez
SIBLINGS/Sisters, Sharon and Anna Ramirez
WIFE/None
CHILDREN/None
EMERGENCY CONTACT IN THE EVENT OF DEATH
    OR GRAVE MEDICAL CONDITION . . . ? `

The atmosphere of the place was still settling over me like a lead balloon so I hadn't noticed the break in her chatter.

Mr. Ramirez, who is your emergency contact?

Oh! My father is my emergency contact, I offered. She asked me for a phone number where he could be reached in the event of an emergency, but I balked at the thought of alarming my father if there ever was an emergency.

Can I get back to you on that? I asked.

Your life, she shot back without a hint of care. Having no need to discuss further the detail of what should happen to me if an emergency involving my death or grave medical condition should arise, she continued on with her battery of questions:

IN THE EVENT OF INCAPACITATION /DNR
ALLERGIES /None
PROSTHETICS /None

No major surgeries, no history of asthma, no known heart conditions, no history of cancer, gonorrhea, chlamydia, syphilis, HIV/AIDS, moderate substance abuse: including marijuana, PCP, alcohol—

No alcohol, I interjected.

No alcohol, she repeated tersely before continuing her rapid-fire recitation:

Mixed-Personality Disorder, with Passive-Aggressive
Features; no history of depression, no history of psychotic
episodes or psych meds, no extensive history of violence—

Is there anything I missed? She asked flatly.

I felt more naked at her interview than when I was in front of the stern-faced lieutenant. This woman who knew nothing of me other than an administrative report had drawn whatever conclusions she had and had asked me not to interrupt. I felt defeated.

One more question, Mr. Ramirez: Race—white or Black?

Her question caught me off guard, as it had never occurred to me that I had to be one or the other. I couldn't ever remember attaching any real significance to race. I remembered the naïve way that I thought racism was a thing of the past; I would tell my friends that I looked forward to the day when we would live without categorization, when we would no longer be Black, White, Latino, Asian, man, woman, rich, poor, uptown, downtown, gay, straight .... We would be human beings, a family. However, the immediate reality suggested something altogether different.

My journey up to this point had been knocking down my idealistic beliefs in justice and the American way of opportunity being available to all. The sea of brown and black faces among which I was awash, the cresting waves of nihilism that beat on our psyche day after day, was awakening some genetically encoded feeling of inferiority. If left unchecked this pragmatism would drown any optimism left in me. I knew I was in hell, a place that would make every attempt to tear kindness apart; cruel and unapologetic. This place would reduce men to animals: predator and prey; it would make nightmares real and cherished memories fade into doubt. Here prayers would go unanswered because here there is no God. But that is the aim of hell: to rob the strong and hopeful of their strength and hope.

The ironic thing about hell is that it does present its denizens with a choice: give in to the hate and pity, or outwit the devil by fighting with all of your nerve and sinew until fighting becomes as reflexive as breathing. Of course, you can never let the devil know you're fighting, and, above all, you can never let him know you're winning.

All of these emotions ran through me in a split second as I considered the nurse's question. I could be White and it wouldn't matter to anyone—I would still be a prisoner. Or I could be Black and quietly live with the confidence that I went against someone's plan.

Mr. Ramirez, what's it gonna be—White or Black?

Her impatience brought me back to the moment. With a flush coming over me I responded with the urgency of a self-imposed mute who has waited for the perfect moment to speak:

Black ....

I let the word trail off my tongue as if it were the answer to an ageless riddle that I had just figured out. A soft smile pulled at the corners of my lips and I watched as her pen stumbled on the page. I saw the clouds of confusion darken her skies. I never was one to do as expected, and my defiance perplexed her just enough that I knew I had steered her into uncharted territory. Her expression said it all: *How could this fair-skinned, straight-haired man not be white?* She was the one putting a premium on her whiteness, not me. I valued stuffing her smugness back in her face.

It would be a few years before the D.O.C. would correct that bit of information, for census data or whatever. But on that day I was assigned to a dusty cell with a sweat-stained mattress, and I slept well. My introduction into hell had worn down every muscle in my body. But in the blackness of night a Black man slept, victorious—if only in a small way—and optimistic that winning was possible.

Aaron C. W.

CONSPIRACY

To Chester Children-at-Risk

I've been asked to write something for *children-at-risk* in Chester, Pennsylvania,[1] and I wanted to give you something real, because I know that *scared straight stuff* doesn't work, as a father of six, grandfather of six and from my personal experience.

As a child, I went to a *scared-straight sort of program at Corwell Heights*, the roughest juvenile lock-up in the United States, in the seventies. The more people told me I wouldn't make it, that I would be some man's piece of butt or sex object, the more I became obsessed with proving each one of them wrong. The more I wanted to prove I could make it in the roughest joint there is, while staying in one piece throughout the entire ordeal, and at the time of my departure. So, I later ended up at the YSC,[2] Abraxas,[3] Corwell Heights Security Unit A,[4] Holmesburg Prison B-Block,[5] the Detention Center (B-Block),[6] PICC (J-Block and G-2),[7] SCI-Camp Hill (A-Block and J-Block),[8] SCI-

---

[1] This was written for Widener University Professor Jayne Thompson's creative writing class.

[2] Former Youth Study Center, Phila., PA.

[3] Marienville, PA, a last-stop juvenile lock-up before Corwell Heights Security Unit.

[4] The roughest juvenile lock-up in the United States, and the roughest unit in Corwell Heights Security Unit.

[5] Holmesburg Prison, Phila., PA, B-Block, way in the back of the block.

[6] Philadelphia Detention Center, County Prison, and B-Block are for violent offenders, murderers, etc., where on my first day I observed two prisoners dragging a homosexual in the cell to rape him. I hadn't even made it to my cell with my bed roll yet.

[7] Philadelphia Industrial Correctional Center, Phila., PA, and J-Block is the hole block, but G-2 is the second wildest block in the prison to J-Block.

[8] SCI-Camp Hill is Classification for PA State prisons.

Frackville (7-Block later changed to A-Block),[9] and SCI-Graterford (E-block and D-block).[10]

In each jail, they always housed me on the toughest block, way in the back of the block, where it was like they wanted something to happen to me, but nothing happened to me. I just kept on surviving and am still surviving, after spending over 23 years of my 42 years of life in prison, and one jail cell after another. So, I know the *scared-straight stuff* doesn't work from *firsthand experience.*

The thing I've decided to give you is called *"Conspiracy!"* It's something real and I must admit when I was young, running around and acting a fool, I didn't have a true understanding of it. But when it's responsible for taking your life away from you, for the last 20 years, you try your hardest to make some sense of it, to try to understand it, but in the end of all your thinking and understanding, it still does not make any sense!

As a child, it was hard accepting responsibility for the dumb stuff I did. When they told me 20 years ago, at the age of 22, that my life was being taken away from me, for something someone I was with had done, and something I had nothing to do with, it was a hard, bitter and sour pill for me to swallow, then and still now, 20 years later.

Let me explain what I am talking about when I say, "Conspiracy." You and I were going to hang out at the mall. You know, do some shoplifting or some of that *new flash mob stuff.* We show up at Footlocker, and it's *18 other kids* there for a *flash mob snatch-and-grab.* We enter Footlocker, bum rush the store, *20 deep,* snatching sneakers, sweat suits and jerseys from racks and shelves, before breaking out the door. *One of the 18 people*—you don't know—brings a gun, and during the *flash mob snatch-and-grab*, shoots and kills a store employee, who was trying to stop him from fleeing the store with the items he had snatched.

Do you know what the charge is going to be *for all 20 of us?*

[9] SCI-Frackville is the State prison where disciplinary prisoners are sent coming out of the SMU for a 2-year probationary period, before being sent to another State prison, if successful; and 7-Block is the roughest block in the prison.

[10] SCI-Graterford is the 4th largest maximum security prison in the United States with a notorious reputation for violence, rapes, stabbings, extortion and occasional killings. The roughest block in the prison is D-Block, with E-Block coming in a close 2nd to D-Block.

MURDER!

So, okay what we were doing was criminal, but do you know the penalty that will be sought *for all 20 of us*, children-at-risk, some in trouble previously, some not?

Death (Capital Murder) or its runner-up, life imprisonment, which in this state is called ***DBI: DEATH BY INCARCERATION!*** You remain in prison until you die, regardless of whether it takes 10, 20, 30, or 50 years for that death to occur. You remain in prison. *No parole! No commutation! No going home!*

We went out to have what we considered a little "fun," do some *flash mob snatch-and-grab stuff.* You know, get some free (stolen) sneakers, sweat suits and jerseys.

We didn't know any of the other 18 people.

We didn't know one of the 18 had a gun.

We didn't know one of the 18 was going to shoot and kill someone.

We didn't plan to shoot anyone, let alone kill anyone.

We don't own any guns; have never carried any guns or shot any guns before.

Do you know some of the 18 will get a deal of third-degree murder to testify against the others, but with our prior school and juvenile records of being in trouble with the school, our parents, the neighborhood and law, it won't be us? Because of that we don't have any character witnesses who testify about our reputation in the Community!

The difference in Pennsylvania, between first-degree murder,[11] second-degree murder,[12] and third-degree murder,[13] is with first degree, if the State doesn't kill you, you remain in prison for the rest of your natural life, as you will if you're convicted of second-degree murder. Whereas if you're convicted of third-degree murder, after 10, 20, or more years of imprisonment, you'll be allowed to return home. *However, in this flash mob snatch-and-grab killing incident,* **the majority of the 20 of us, including me, are going to jail for life!**

---

[11] First-degree murder is a premeditated murder.

[12] Second-degree murder is a killing committed during the commission or attempt to commit a felony, such as robbery or the flash mob snatch and grab incident.

[13] Third-degree murder is a killing committed in the heat of passion.

In Pennsylvania, when you get life, it means life. That's until the actual day you die of natural causes, the day someone kills you, or the day you become so fed up with all the nonsense you decide to take your own life.

In Pennsylvania, there are about 5,000 prisoners sentenced to life imprisonment in State prison. Many people believe that all 5,000 of those lifers are murderers, killers, and that they have actually committed and performed the act of murder. *But that's not true! Less than half of the 5,000 people serving a sentence of life is guilty of actually taking a person's life. The remaining portion of persons sentenced to life imprisonment are serving life as conspirators, accomplices, aiders and abettors, and have never taken a life before, but are serving life imprisonment as many of the 20 of us will be serving under my first example, the flash mob snatch-and-grab gang killing.*

If the *flash mob snatch-and-grab shooting and killing* example did not get your attention about this thing called "Conspiracy," here below is another example about "Sammy."

Let's say that you and Sam are best buddies. You go everywhere together and do everything together. You and Sam have even experimented with drugs and petty crimes, such as boosting (i.e., shoplifting), burglary, auto theft and fighting (assault). Then one day on your way to school, Sam shows you a gun he took out of his big brother's room, without his big brother's consent or knowledge.

You and Sam head to an alley by the school. It's an alley where all the kids hang out, and do all the things we both know kids should not be doing. You begin setting up empty bottles and crushed beer and soda cans on the broken down wall of an abandoned house in the alley. You and Sam then take turns firing the gun, trying to hit the empty bottles and crushed beer and soda cans off the abandoned house's broken down wall.

It's almost time for first period, so you and Sam head for the school with the gun tucked away in Sam's waistband and under his sweatshirt.

Before you and Sam reach the school, you both step in the candy store, like the two of you have done previously, on every school morning in the past. But this morning, it is different.

When you and Sam reach the counter to pay for your chips and soda, you hand the cashier, Mr. Bob, a $5 bill to pay for your purchase and while Mr. Bob has the cash register open, Sam pulls out the gun and tells Mr. Bob to put all the money in a brown paper bag.

Mr. Bob refuses and tries to tell Sammy not to do this. You say nothing. You have no gun. You don't go get the money from the cash register. You don't attempt to help Mr. Bob, you don't tell Sam not to do what he is doing, nor do you attempt to help Sam. Mr. Bob then tries to take the gun from Sammy, and is fatally shot during the struggle over the gun. You hear the gunshot and instinct kicks in and you flee the store, heading for school, because you can't go home until after 3 o'clock, when school lets out.

Sam flees the store right after you and passes the gun to Ant, who you both bump into during your run to school. Ant agrees to hold the gun until 3 o'clock, not knowing anything about Mr. Bob, the shooting or your and Sam's presence in Mr. Bob's store.

By lunchtime, the police are at the school and have you and Sam in custody, charging both of you as adults, with capital murder, robbery and other offenses relating to Sam's impulsively pulling out the gun, his apparently unpremeditated shooting and killing of the store owner, Mr. Bob, during a failed robbery attempt. Apparently he saw all that cash and pulled out the gun on impulse, thought the very sight of it would get Mr. Bob to hand over the money, didn't ever follow his thoughts through to where he might kill anybody.

The state is seeking the death penalty and/or a sentence of life imprisonment for you and Sam, if convicted. *Remember in PA life is life, until you actually die, are killed, or kill yourself, and that's regardless of whether it takes 20 years or 50 years. It is no going home!*

At trial, the State puts on witnesses who testify that you and Sammy were shooting a gun in the alley prior to school on the morning Mr. Bob was shot and killed. You know taking target practice on crushed beer and soda cans are signs of premeditation and first-degree-murder.

Witnesses testify they heard a gunshot coming from Mr. Bob's store, and then observed you and Sammy running from Mr. Bob's store, shortly after hearing the gunshot.

Ant testifies that Sam gave him a gun after the shooting to hold for him until after school, 3 o'clock. He then testifies that you and Sam went to school together, after Sam gave him the gun. Of course, Ant is facing charges for possession of the weapon and needs help on his own legal woes from the State.

Are you guilty of murder under these circumstances? How about robbery? You never said nor did anything! But you're on trial for your life!

You refuse to testify against Sammy because you are best buddies, grew up together, know each other's family, spent the night and ate at each other's home and dinner table. You know each other's mother, girlfriend and children. How could you ever look those people in the eye again if you testified against Sammy and sent him to prison for life or to death row, for the State to kill your best buddy? You don't think about the fact that when Sammy pulled the gun on Mr. Bob, he was involving you in a crime, endangering your life. You only think about his being your 'friend' and keep your mouth shut.

You and Sammy are convicted of second-degree-murder and sentenced to a mandatory term of life imprisonment. Your life as you know it is now over, even though you've never actually shot, never actually killed, and never actually robbed anyone. You were only guilty of keeping your mouth shut. You're now being held responsible and punished for the actions of your best buddy, Sammy.

It's hard for any human, child or adult to accept responsibility for their own actions, wrongs and faults, but now the law says you are responsible not only for your own actions, but the actions of another, like *your best buddy Sammy, or the one in the 20 flash mob snatch-and-grab gang shooting and killing example.*

From the day that Mr. Bob was shot and killed, you and Sammy were and will always be described as killers, murderers and robbers in any records read, media announcements and stories told about either one of you, regardless of what you go on to do and achieve, in life, and for many, many years after your actual death.

So what I want to give you is "Conspiracy!" I want for you to agree to walk away from a crowd, a best buddy, a classmate or a neighborhood friend when they say they're about to do some dumb stuff, because you never know how that dumb stuff will turn out, and that dumb stuff might cost you your actual life. Don't get caught up in this "Conspiracy" web that has eaten the lives of over 3,000 men, women and children in PA, who have been sitting in a cage for decades waiting to die, waiting for someone to kill them, or waiting to take their own lives. Conspiracy is deadly, especially when you haven't taken a life, but your life is actually taken!

You weren't created to live in a cage—no human or creature was—nor experience any of the inhumane, torturous, cruel, rotten and ill treatment that you are subjected to, and experience when living in these cages on a daily basis. Each generation is responsible for the successes and failures of the next generation. When I see a child, the next generation being brought on the housing unit to live with me, I am reminded of how I have failed the next generation, by my absence over the last 20 years. I was supposed to be there to teach you, to support you, to show you I care and to help you be successful, and all that you can be, in this life. But my advice, support, love, care and words come from a tip of a pen, rather than my physical presence. So, I truly do apologize to each one of you, and to all children, for walking away from you, my responsibility!

I want you to know, as long as you have life in your body, you have the chance to write the next page and chapter in your book of life. They may classify you as a child-at-risk today, but tomorrow they can classify you as the most powerful political figure, Fortune 500 CEO, or Community Giant that the world has ever known. You can go on to be great, make powerful contributions to society like Martin Luther King, Malcolm X, President Obama, Roxanne Jones, Lucien Blackwell, David Richardson, Harriet Tubman, or any other person that has sacrificed so much of his or her own life, for us to have the opportunities that are being taken away from us, and you, today, on a daily basis. Think about it for a moment: we have people who have died, just for you to have the right to go to school. Today, our elected officials and so-called leaders are closing schools and merging those same schools, because they say they have no money to keep these schools open. However, these same elected officials and so-called leaders have money any day of the week for a new $200 million prison—as they've done for the 20 prisons built in the last 40 years—compared to not one $200 million school—nor any school—being built in Pennsylvania during the same 40-year time-period. Those people who gave their lives so that you and I can go to school are probably turning over in their graves, right now!

Just because they built a cell for you, when you were in 4th grade, at recess and learning math, you don't have to occupy that cell! You have the next generation to care for, which, after all, will be your very own child(ren) and seed. Don't fail them, like I've failed you, by my absence!

Take this life I am giving you today, and pass it on to your mother and sister, your father and brother, your neighbor and friend, your child and their child.

Don't fall into that trap called 'Conspiracy!'

Harun F.

BETRAYAL

I've been in a gang since I was twelve years old. One day when I was fifteen, I went around to another member's house. He wasn't home, but his people said he was at another member's house around the corner. I went there and knocked on the door. One of the crew answered and let me in. I asked for "Datie," and he said everyone was upstairs in the front bedroom. As I climbed the stairs, though the door was closed, I could hear laughter and talk coming from the bedroom. I smiled to myself as I thought, *They must have already bought some wine. I hope I'm not too late.*

I tapped on the door and opened it without waiting for a response. Datie was sitting in the right hand corner, facing the window in a chair clutching a gallon of Italian Swiss Colony dark tokay between his legs. He shouted out to me to come on over and have a taste. I made my way through the crowd, slapping palms, giving hugs and greetings. When I got to Datie, I took the keg of wine and went up. I swallowed about half a quart before bringing it down.

I needed to get drunk immediately. As I stood there talking to Datie, I began to feel trapped. In the midst of all of this was a girl lying on the bed, naked. I knew her. She was about 13, but she was big for her age. She looked more like 16 or 17. She was just lying there, seemingly oblivious to the whole situation. I wanted to break and run, but knew I couldn't. Finally Datie told me, "Go ahead and get you some." I felt like the whole world was looking at me and my reaction would validate or undermine my manhood and status. All the while, this was something I really, really didn't want to do. I'd never done it before. I thought about how disgusted I felt when I heard dudes talking about how they "pulled a train" on some girl. Now here I was in the middle of one. My hesitation was becoming obvious as a voice from somewhere in the room called out "Go ahead man!" I looked in her face as I walked towards the bed. She gave no indication that she cared one way or the other about the situation. I took my hat and jacket off and handed them to someone.

I always felt that I betrayed myself in this situation for not having the courage to stand on what I believed in and walk away. I am 69 years old, and those memories still haunt me today.

Kempis S.

ABSENCE OF LIGHT

Sean Johnson, a.k.a. Lil' Sean, was 15 years old when he was arrested for his involvement in a robbery-turned-homicide. He was the only minor in the company of three young adults, 18, 19, and 21, when they all entered a pawn shop with intentions to rob the place. During the episode, a struggle ensued between the shop owner and one of the robbers, a gunshot was heard, and the owner lay motionless on the floor. The robbers fled the scene, but were rounded up not long afterward, with the help of eyewitnesses. Even though evidence showed that Lil' Sean was not the shooter, that he did not have a gun, and he testified that he did not know that one of his friends had a gun or that someone would get shot, he was convicted of First Degree Murder and sentenced, at the age of 16, to life without parole (LWOP). He would be sent to the adult prison system to serve out that sentence.

Lil' Sean was a handsome teenage boy, not physically imposing, somewhat frail, perhaps from undernourishment. And today, he was especially aware of his own slightness, as he sat handcuffed and shackled on the prison bus, pulling up to what he believed would be a cruel place, crowded with big, strong, muscle-bound, and mean criminals who could each easily dwarf and overpower him. He decided he had to exaggerate his size and bearing some kind of way, to make himself seem bigger and less approachable than he actually was. He stepped off the bus onto the prison grounds with his flat back straightened, his chicken chest inflated and pushed out, and his baby face as grim as he could make it. "I'm no-nonsense, don't mess with me" was the illusion he wanted to cast. He strolled as thuggishly as the shackles around his ankles would allow. His effort was conspicuous to some of the other felons on the bus, and to the receiving guards.

To all of them it was all more sad than humorous because they knew the harsh realities that awaited Sean behind those 40-ft. high concrete walls. And they knew that he knew it too, and that he was preparing to survive. They had to respect that. But they also knew from their own seasonings, as convicts or guards in the system, that his efforts would be to little effect. For his mask was more Mad Puppy than Mad Dog. Truth is, the kid was never more full of anxiety than he was at the moment, from all the dreadful jail-tales and stereotypes about convicts he had heard while growing up in the hood. He never actually anticipated this day, however, when he, himself, would be actually entering this very place of frightening legend as a convicted robber/murderer.

After processing was completed, a guard led the line of 21 newly arrived convicts on the long walk to the housing area. They each wore orange jumpsuits indicating their status as new arrivals, and they each carried a small cardboard records box containing a basic state issue of hygienic items, and a linen set-up. Once again, Lil' Sean was the only minor in the bunch. To him, the march through the long prison hallway was a long slow-motion run through a gauntlet of unnerving stares. Some eyes were merely curious, while others scanned the convoy for a familiar face, a family member or neighborhood friend. And yet, others searched the herd for potential quarry…, the hungriest of which, having a perverted taste for youthful innocence, naiveté, and vulnerability, zeroed in on Lil' Sean. Fresh young meat.

When Lil' Sean stepped on to his assigned cell-block, the booty bandits fixed their gazes on him like birds of prey. They put their most lustful faces on while grabbing their crotches. Their perverted gazes invaded the boy's jumpsuit, sizing up their prize, and revving themselves up to arrest the budding manhood of another child condemned by society and the system. Lil' Sean felt naked and already violated.

He slid open the cell door, stepped in, flipped-up the light switch, and illuminated what was basically a filthy 6 x 10 ft. bathroom with a steel bunk bed and steel desk in it. Lil' Sean wasn't even sure if he was up to the task of cleaning it. He didn't even want to look at it right now. He sat his box down on the desk, clicked the light back off, and sat on the edge of the bunk. He was confused. *How did I end up here?* he asked himself. *Why me? How and how long am I going to make it in this place?* His mind was desperately trying to resuscitate a hope that just wasn't responding. His days may well be numbered, he thought.

He searched his memory for faces and names of refuge, support and comfort, but found no one and nothing that represented love and concern for him…except his mother…who died of AIDS when he was 5 years old. He never heard anything good about her. "Your mother was a drug addict. She didn't even know who your father was." It was as if everyone who came into his life tried to chase his love for his mother out of his heart. But she was the only one who had ever loved him. If it wasn't for her, he would never have had any love in his life at all.

She loved him so much that he never saw her flaws. He would never stop loving her. It was her face that made him become so talented and exquisite with pencils, paintbrushes, pastels, and poetry. Nearly all of his sketched or painted portraits were of his mother's beautiful face and heavenly smile. It was as if he was trying to bring her back to life through his craft, so lifelike was his work. And it was all from memory. He had no photograph of her. Or perhaps he was trying to recapture, to give himself the warmth, the peace, the love and affection, the security, the sense of worth that he remembered her face and smile always giving him.

Lil' Sean had grown accustomed to loneliness. It was one of his constant companions, along with neglect, abuse, and nightmares from the age of 5, when he was placed in the foster care system and shuffled from one foster home to another, up to the time of his arrest. They were such die-hard companions that they even followed him here.

Lil' Sean didn't have a penny to his name. He was hungry, he needed a pair of sneakers; the prison boots, which had no arch, were killing his feet. He had no family or friends on the outside, no one to call for support in these dark and dismal hours. The only family he had ever known, or at least that he thought he had, was Ty, Slim, and Calvin, his gang members who were now convicted felons for the pawn shop robbery homicide. That illusion was blown to smithereens when Calvin, who was actually the shooter, lied to the police about his three friends and copped a plea for a 20 to 40 year sentence. Calvin said he'd rather do numbers than letters (LIFE). This reminded Lil' Sean of his fifth lifelong companion: Betrayal.

He had been in the cell for only 10 minutes, but Lil' Sean was already understanding more with each passing second, each thought, the nature of his situation: he was a Lifer, a Juvenile Lifer, and he may be raped or hurt very badly real soon. He couldn't even imagine himself being raped, having such a violation committed against him, and possibly even being given AIDS. But he knew he would have to face the booty bandits all too soon, because they were surely already planning their movements to come into contact with him.

From his position, sitting on his bunk, Lil' Sean could see two guys who weren't there before now posted up on the opposite tier, directly across from his cell, apparently engaged in conversation, while cutting deliberate glances into his cell, at him.

How would I fight them off when they come? Should I even try? Would I make it worse on myself by fighting? But what could be worse than being raped, and maybe catching AIDS? Will they stab me? What can I use to defend myself? Lil' Sean's confidence was straining under the weight of these questions.

And it bore down on him heavier and heavier what his sentence to LWOP meant. It meant that he was never going to be free ever again. It meant that he would never become the renowned artist, poet, and writer that he had always dreamed of becoming. It meant that he was sent to this unforgiving place to die by lethal environment. Period.

Lil' Sean thought about his mom and how much he missed her and wished that she, or anyone, were here for him. But it was when he thought about tomorrow, that his face collapsed into his hands and for the first time in quite a few of his young years, the floodgates that were frozen shut long ago inside him, opened up. He couldn't hold back the tears any longer. Life had made a cruel habit of breaking this child's heart.

Suddenly, the light coming in through the doorway disappeared and a huge shadow was cast into the cell. Lil' Sean, still sitting on the edge of his bunk with his face in his hands, felt the sudden absence of light…or the sudden presence of darkness…or both. He lifted his face from his hands, turned his head and looked up towards a larger man standing in his doorway … .

Termaine J. H.

S.T.E.P.U.P

I believe now is the time for us, as children of God, to STEP UP and say no to bullies, become the voice for our brothers and sisters who have been stifled by this debilitating culture.

S.T.E.P.U.P. (Selfless Thinking Expresses Potential that Uplifts People) is an acronym that I coined in response to this prevalent issue with the hope of giving victims of bullies and violence a platform to stand on, letting them know that they're not alone. Bullying and violence are related. A person being bullied can only take so much before they strike back with some form of violence. It could be directed towards the source of the bullying—the victim can wake up one morning and explode in a rage of violence against the perpetrators of the bullying. Or it could be directed at a group of innocent people: the students at Columbine, for instance.

Most importantly, victims could commit acts of violence against themselves. There could be self-cutting just to transfer the emotional pain that they're suffering to physical pain. It can even get as violent and tragic as suicide. Rutgers student Tyler Clemente and countless others are examples.

We have to be vigilant because bullies don't always physically or openly beat on people. They also beat victims down verbally, calling them all types of names. They've even begun to use cyberspace. Bullies would take a friendly picture that you've sent for your friends only, and expose it to hundreds, if not thousands, of people. Or bullies can simply refuse to allow a person to become a part of their clique because of a person's look, style, race, or gender. Bullies also come in all shapes, sizes, and ages. They're in every school, grade, neighborhood, and place of employment. Perhaps there's one sitting, standing, or working next to you right now.

Why do bullies bully? There are many reasons. They may have

been bullied once themselves or have a fear of being alone or disliked. Perhaps they do it to be accepted, or they may just want attention. Whatever the case, S.T.E.P.U.P.'s goal is to enable the world with a courageous type of selflessness to prevent bullying altogether. Sure, it's never been popular to S.T.E.P.U.P. and speak for someone, especially someone being bullied. You have a rep to protect. You can't be seen helping someone being bullied. Better him than you, right? Wrong.

What if you were the one who just transferred to a new school, neighborhood, or job and didn't know anyone? What if you were the one who was not allowed to be a part of a clique? What if you were the one nobody talked to? What if you were the one being backed into a corner, having your personal property violated and taken from you and you're left alone, paralyzed with what I call the "three crippling emotions": fear, anxiety, and depression? What if it was your little sisters, brothers, best friends, parents, grandparents, or children being bullied and you weren't there to help them? You'd want somebody to S.T.E.P.U.P. and say, "No. Not on my watch. Not right now. Not ever," right? Well, it starts with you. It only takes one person to S.T.E.P.U.P. and say no.

I believe you have the power to be the world's greatest surveillance system by becoming your brothers' and sisters' keepers. You have the cure to eradicate this cancer called "Bullies." The next time you see people being bullied—struggling with the "three crippling emotions": fear, anxiety, and depression—stand next to them. Put your hand around their shoulder, letting them know that they're not alone, silently saying to bullies, "No. Not on my watch. Not right now. Not ever."

Former President Calvin Coolidge, the 30th President of the United States, said, "We cannot do everything at once, but we can all do something at once." I believe if we all S.T.E.P.U.P. at once, then bullies don't stand a chance.

Razzaqq G.

ESCAPING THE DARK ME

"I'm pregnant."

These two words changed my life over and over again, particularly because I was only twelve years old. What did I know about being a father? I mean what model did I have? My father was a deadbeat who ran away from his responsibility at the ripe age of nineteen. If he couldn't be a father at nineteen, what could I do at such a young age?

I didn't exactly *not* have a good model for a father. My grandfather replaced my father and was the best dad I could have ever asked for. Being raised by my grandparents was a gift. I can imagine how I would have turned out if I would have stayed with my drug-addicted mother, or my immature father. So, I could just do what my grandfather did and I'd be alright.

Looking down at the ground outside of my South Philly home, Laura interlocked her small pale fingers and asked, "How we gonna afford to take care of it?"

My anxiety mirrored hers. Chewing my nails, I looked into two beautiful blue eyes, glossy and trembling.

"I guess I gotta get a job," I said. I studied Laura's face, looking to see if my words had calmed her. Her eyes lifted a little higher as she stepped up to me, wrapping her slim arms around my waist. I may have calmed her nerves some, but little did she know that mine were speeding around my body like cars on a highway.

So, I did get a job that year, working under the table for a Burger King. All they let me do was take out the trash. They didn't pay me much, but with the help of my grandparents and Laura's adopted mother we made it.

Two years after my beautiful Brianna was born, I was working part time at the same Burger King, trying to make it easy for my new family. That July, I heard the same two words that I thought I wouldn't hear again for years. "I'm pregnant."

"What!" I exclaimed, pacing the floor of my house. I walked back and forth for so long it looked like the carpet was wearing down right before my eyes. After a similar conversation to the first, we went to sleep that night knowing that we'd get through it.

But it wasn't as easy with two kids. It put me and my family in a bad place for a while, so Laura mentioned looking for a job. I didn't like that; I wanted her to be home with the kids. I felt like it was my duty to take care of them all.

So you can imagine how I responded when Dang approached me with "an offer I couldn't refuse." I met Dang through my brother Charles, who had always been into the streets. Charles shot and killed somebody when he was twelve and went away to juvie for eight years. We stayed close while he was in juvie. I went to see him when my mom showed up to take me along to visit him. Shortly before my son Antonio was born, Charles was released from juvie and got right back into the street life. His homie Dang had maintained contact with him and set him right up in "The Game" when he got home.

One day I got a call from Dang. "Yo, Lil' C. I'm tryna holla at you. You busy right now?" I never really liked that he called me Lil' C, short for little Charles.

Narrowing my eyes, I looked at the phone receiver and said, "My name's Raz, not Charles."

"A'ight, a'ight," he responded. I could see him on the other end, securing the phone to his shoulder, leaning his head to the side, and then holding his hands up in the air as if submitting. But I should have known he wasn't submitting; he had an agenda. "How bout Raz; I know C call you that."

"That's cool," I said, and it was; that's what most people called me anyway.

"So is you busy now?" He repeated his initial question.

"Nah," I responded.

"I'll be there in like fifteen."

I had no clue what he wanted to talk to me about, and for some reason I was nervous. It wasn't like I had never met him. I kind of looked up to him. I admired how confident and take charge he was. He had a presence you couldn't ignore. I heard him a few times talking on his phone as he conducted his business and I found myself listening intently to him like I was listening to a new hit song on the radio.

Fifteen minutes after I hung up the phone, Dang was walking through my door. My eyes widened as I took in his old school style. I checked out his snake skin shoes, black slacks and his powder blue dress shirt open, showing a gold Italian link chain hanging over a tank top. He sat on the sofa, pulling out a silver cigarette case. He flipped the it open, revealing a row of Newports, and held it out to me. I took one and he followed, shutting it as he put the cigarette in his mouth. I pulled a plastic lighter from my pocket and lit mine, watching as he lit his with a expensive-looking butane lighter.

"You want somethin' to drink?" I asked him.

"Nah, man. I ain't gonna be long." He wiped sweat from his dark-skinned forehead with his hand and then rubbed it on his pants. "Listen," he started as I sat down across from him. "I know you got them kids now. That lil' job you got can't be helpin' with them."

"It's alright work, especially for a fifteen year old."

"Nigga, when I was fifteen I was drivin' a Caddie and eatin' at five star restaurants." I knew he wasn't exaggerating. I heard my brother talk about how good Dang always had been in the "game." Two streams of smoke flew from his nostrils as he smashed the butt of his cigarette into the ashtray.

"I ain't gonna make this long. Your brother say you real smart. I can tell you are, too, just from bein' round you. If you want some work, I got somethin' for you."

"What kind of work you talkin' bout?"

"You know what kind, my man. You already got the tools; you smart, your brother said he showed you how to shoot a gun, and I done heard about some of them rumbles you been in. Nigga, you got it, you just got to use it."

I thought about it for what seemed like hours, but seeing as though Dang couldn't stay long, I doubt it was more than a minute. Nodding my head, I finally said, "A'ight. What I gotta do?"

So he brought me into his "empire." Among many other things

he ran what he called a "titty house" in a couple different towns around the Philly area. Provided with a 9 millimeter and a .45, all I had to do was make sure stuff didn't go wrong when men came in to see the girls.

I saw a lot of things in that house. It probably changed how I viewed the world all together. I saw men beaten, women beaten, gang bangs, and other things that you would only think you could see in a porno movie. Eventually some of the beatings were handed out by me. I pistol whipped men for mistreating the women and smacked around the girls when they tried to skim some of their earnings. I always looked at Dang as the pimp; he owned the place. But me and the other guys he hired to run the place—the middle management—we were the pimps.

Funny thing was, my family never knew what I had gotten into, except for my brother. To them I was a loving teenage father of two who took care of them and their mother. They all still thought I was working at Burger King. Well, I kind of was. I decreased my hours, but they thought I was still working close to full time. Laura never questioned where the extra money was coming from. She assumed I got a raise or two. So, at home I cooked dinner with my family, cleaned the house, watched movies, and changed diapers. Outside of the home, I had become dangerous; I had become ruthless, just like Dang.

I don't think Laura would have ever believed that the same hands that gently caressed her soft milky skin, played games with our children, prepared romantic Valentine's Day dinners for two, could ever be the same hands that would shoot a man in the face, or beat a woman with the back of a gun. They didn't suspect that when it came to making money, or demanding my respect, I became someone else.

About two years after I started working for Dang, I got into an incident in the "titty house." I was sitting on a grey beat up couch we kept downstairs, when I heard one of the girls upstairs yelling. I grabbed the .45 from my waist and ran upstairs. Screams reached my ears as I heard struggling through a door down the hall.

I kicked in the door and stared down at blood staining the light blue carpet, turning a small circular dark spot purple. I quickly scanned the room, my gaze falling on Tracey, one of our girls, naked, curled up against the white wall. Standing over her was a tall, slim, brown-skinned man, raising his hand to strike her. I raised the gun, pointed it at Slim's head and yelled, "Yo!" Whipping his head around, he glared at me with pure rage and hate. I don't know what happened before I got there, but it didn't matter. It was time to do my job. He turned toward me and took one step before I put a hole through his right shoulder.

Grabbing his shoulder he dropped to one knee and yelled something inaudible. He looked back up at me and said, "Nigga, you shot me."

I ignored the obvious and stared coldly at him, face blank, pressing the barrel of the gun to the top of his head. "Get out. Come back and the next bullet goin' through your head."

He nodded, standing up, as I lowered the gun to my side. He walked to the door and looked back. "You shouldn't have done that, my man. You gonna die for that." And he was gone.

This was one of many incidents in that place, so naturally I didn't tell Dang and just ignored the threat. Foolish. About two weeks later I was walking down the street with Laura who held Antonio, my two year old son, in her arms, and Brianna, now four, holding tightly to my hand.

Two men, one brown-skinned and the other light-skinned were walking toward us, talking, doing nothing out of the ordinary. Funny thing was, I didn't even recognize Slim until he had a gun in my face. "I told you, you shouldn't have messed wit me, nigga."

My skin trembled as goose bumps spread across my entire body. Instinctively I shoved Laura and the kids behind me. CRACK! A skull crushing pain rushed through my body as I fell to one knee, blood trickling into my eyes. Shaking my head, the stars that danced around in my eyes began to dissipate. Suddenly I could hear the cries from both my children and Laura. "It's okay," she whispered to them quietly. "Daddy's okay." I looked up at the barrel of the gun that had just smacked against my head, rattling my brain. Slim pointed the gun at my face, ready to fire. "Wait," I said through panicked breaths. "Not in front of my kids." I allowed my eyes to show him how much I was begging him not to kill me right in front of my family. It seemed to work. He looked up at them and then back at me. I watched in fear as he raised the gun over his head and brought it down across my face, one more time, before running off, with his friend behind him.

I lay on the ground, tears in my eyes. Laura was immediately on her knees, holding my head while still holding on to Antonio. Brianna kneeled beside me and held my hand tightly in hers as tears flowed down her chubby cheeks.

With the initial fear beginning to wear off, and the surety of my family's physical safety, my racing heart started to produce blood-filled rage through my body. I stood up, staring in the direction Slim and his friends had run. I thought about pursuing them, but one look back at Brianna changed my mind. I still felt like my skin was burning hot, and I wanted to destroy what had made me feel this way, but I couldn't leave them there alone.

Laura stepped up to me and placed her hand on my cheek. I stared blankly, as if I could see through her.

"Babe?" she said, confused. I'm not sure what she saw in my face at that moment, but it seemed to frighten her. She attempted to say something, but the words were caught in her throat. I pressed my eyelids tightly together and bit my bottom lip. Just as the copper taste of my own blood touched the tip of my tongue, I opened my eyes again, placing my hand on top of hers, still resting on my cheek.

"It's okay," I said. "Let's go home."

I later found out that was the moment Laura realized there was another person inside of me. She told me on a jail visit that she hadn't known the man on that street, staring blankly into the distance. At the time, my explanation about what had happened was that it had to be a case of mistaken identity, but she didn't buy that. She wasn't sure what had happened, but she started to become curious about what I was out doing when I wasn't with her. I didn't tell her what was going on until I was already in prison.

The next day after the incident, I was still furious. My anger was reinforced by the excruciating headache I had and the lump on the back of my head and side of my face. When we got home, Laura had cleaned the cuts and butterfly stitched them, although I probably needed to go to the hospital.

Early that morning, after I assured Laura I was fine, I drove out to Dang's place. I told him what happened and he seemed just as angry as I was. "Come on, homie," he said. "We gonna get dem niggas!" He grabbed his .45, a can of *Yuengling*, and slid on his black leather jacket. He tugged on a pair of leather gloves so he wouldn't leave any fingerprints on anything. I felt for my .45, secured in the back of my waistband, grabbed another pair of gloves that he had lying on his coffee table, and followed closely behind him. We went to the "house" and asked Tracey if she knew who the man was that attacked her. She told us who he was and where he hung out. That was all the information we needed.

We waited until night and drove around to the area Tracey told us about. I held my gun in my lap, rubbing the butt, anxiety coursing through my blood. We turned a corner and rolled down the block. I could clearly recognize Slim and his friend standing under a street light. There were a few other men around them, so we didn't act right away. We sat in the car for about five minutes before the others left. They were probably copping drugs.

"Ready?" Dang said, gently pressing the gas pedal. Even if I wasn't ready, it was too late now. The spokes on the machine had already started to spin. Before I could answer, we were pulling up right next to them. Slim was standing on the sidewalk on Dang's side of the car and his friend was on the other. This was normal for some hustlers; someone would take the money from one side while another would throw the drugs in the window on the other. Dang rolled his tinted window down halfway as Slim stepped up to the window. "What you need?" he asked.

"Twenty," Dang said, referring to a twenty dollar bag of coke. Without warning, I grasped my .45 and flung open my door, pointing the gun in the face of the man on my side. As he reached for his waist I yelled, "Don't! I'll blow your face off right here!" By the time I turned my gaze to Dang, he was shoving Slim in the back seat of the car, so I followed his lead with the man I held under the aim of my gun. "Get in," I said.

"I ain't gettin' in no car wit y'all." I didn't wait for any other protests. I raised my gun up and brought it down so hard on his head he fell to his knees. I kicked him in the face, forcing him onto his back. As he laid there, blood gushing from his head, I reached for the gun in his belt and patted him down for other weapons. Once I was satisfied he didn't have any I shoved him in the car next to Slim. Dang got in the car and leaned over to the glove box, pulling out a handful of flexi cuffs. Don't ask me why he had them, but I assumed he had done this before. After tying both their hands and ankles, we drove out to a rental storage unit not too far away.

Once inside and out of the car, the scent of stale blood and death assaulted my nostrils. Blood had stained the cement floor. Now I knew Dang had done this before. This was probably a regular spot of his.

Dang stepped around the car and I followed, watching as he walked to the red door tand opened it. We grabbed both men from the back seat and dragged them to the corner of the empty space. This place hadn't been used for storage in quite some time.

"So," Dang started, after he sliced the flexi cuffs off them. "You niggas come to my place of business, damage my merchandise, and try to get at my homie?" Slim's friend started to say something, but before a word came out, a loud bang rang through the room. I flinched, but immediately regained my composure as I looked at the blood rushing from the friend's leg. Dang had shot him once through both legs. My hearing was temporarily impaired, but I could still hear him screaming. Walking over to the man and kneeling beside him, Dang pulled out a knife and pressed it to his throat. "Stop that bitch ass crying 'fore *I* stop it."

The man immediately pressed his lips tightly together, trapping his screams behind them. I looked at Slim, his eyes bulging, lips trembling in fear. I stepped up close to him and shot him in his knee without blinking. He was smart, though. He pressed his lips together and I almost smiled at the muffled girlish sounds escaping his lips.

Adrenaline rushed through my body. I felt like a king. I wanted to do so much more to these two men for disrespecting me in front of my family. They put my kids in danger. The thought of Brianna and Antonio forced my hand to reach for Dang's knife. He let it go with no protest and watched as I knelt next to Slim.

"Put your hand on the ground," I demanded. Slowly, he placed his right hand flat on the cold ground. I plunged the knife down in his hand

and waited for a scream that didn't come. I looked up into his eyes as tears fell down his face.

Not satisfied, I said, "Put the other one down."

"Come on man, please," he begged. I had no mercy for him. I slid the blade of the knife across his cheek, forcing open a wound so deep, some of the blood splattered in my face. "Put it down," I repeated. Shaking uncontrollably, he placed his left hand on the ground as I jammed the knife straight through. He couldn't help the yelp that broke through his clenched teeth.

I stood up and pointed my gun at his head, ready to pull the trigger, when Dang grabbed my shoulder.

"Nah man, they got the point. We ain't killin' nobody tonight." He turned to the two wounded, bloody men and said, "Ya'll get the fuck outta here; I don't care if you got to crawl. We see either of you again, we won't be so merciful next time. Got it?" he asked, looking from one to the other, waiting for a response. The only thing they could do was shake their heads and scurry out of the storage unit, limping and holding each other up.

Standing next to the car, I watched them fall, help one another back up, and rush as quickly as they could, away from us. I still held the knife in my left hand and the gun in my right. Dang stepped up to me and said, "Let's get outta here, man. Leave that here." He nodded his head at my hands. "Somebody'll come clean this up."

We both dropped our guns and I dropped the knife on the ground and then peeled the gloves, soaked with blood, from my hands and dropped them as well. Dang gave me a wet nap and pointed to my face. I wiped blood from my face, and hopped back in the passenger seat of Dang's car.

"Yo, you a bit crazy man," he said, once back on the road.

"What do you mean?"

"Not too many people I know can cut somebody up like that."

For a very brief moment, I looked inside of myself with concern. It worried me that I felt nothing. I was no longer angry, but I wasn't anything else either. I was numb. What had I become in those couple of hours? Was I still me, or was I someone else? I pushed those feelings back down inside of me and stared at the road. I didn't speak for the rest of the ride home.

Things seemed to go right back to normal; me at home as the *me* my family knew, and me on the street as the *me* that people had begun to fear. That lasted only about two months, though. I was in a park with my best friend, Anthony. Ant knew what type of life I was living, but he ran straight with his girlfriend and daughter. He was one of the few friends I had that wasn't into the same things I was. He and I had just finished playing a game of basketball when I noticed two people walking up in black hoodies. I couldn't see their faces, but in my line of "work," I had become very cautious. Realizing I didn't have a gun with me, I told Ant we should walk in the other direction, but before we could get far, the two men ran behind us as I heard gunshots piercing the air of the crowded park. Instinctively, I jumped behind a tree, getting out of the way of the bullets. Then I heard feet pounding into the ground, running away as the bullets stopped. I looked around the tree and my heart skipped a beat as I looked at my friend lying on the ground, blood spilling from his chest.

I ran up to him and dropped to my knees, cradling his head in my arms. That rage that I had become so accustomed to began to boil inside of me. A single tear swelled in my eye, making its way down my cheek. I didn't know what was wrong with me. I thought I was separating my home life from my street life. But was I becoming so cold altogether that I couldn't spare more than one tear for my best friend? Something was wrong with me mentally and I didn't understand what was going on. This time when I questioned myself I didn't push the feelings back down inside of me. I let myself ponder them; I let myself feel them.

Before I could decipher my feelings, my best friend was dead in my arms. The police arrived a few minutes later and questioned me thoroughly. I told them that I had no idea who could have done something like that, but I think they knew I was lying. I went to Dang's and told him about what had taken place in the park. He was up and ready to go after our two assailants in a flash.

"Nah, man," I said to him, sitting on his couch.

His eyes raised in shock. "What?"

I released a deep sigh and said, "I'm tired man."

"A'ight. Go home; we'll get at 'em tomorrow."

"Nah, that ain't what I mean. I'm tired altogether. I can't do this stuff no more."

"Listen, just get some sleep. You just need some rest; you'll be cool tomorrow."

"I won't be cool!" I exclaimed, standing up. I turned my back to him and continued. "I gotta get out. I'm doin' things I never thought I'd be able to do and it's starting to come back home with me. It was cool when this shit didn't follow me home, but now…my main man just got killed because of me. These niggas started this shit in front of my kids…I can't let them get hurt Dang."

Dang looked down at the ground, taking a deep breath. "A'ight," he said lifting his head back up to meet my eyes. "You want out, I got you. You know you not just some nigga that work for me. You like my lil' brother, man…I won't let nothin' happen to you and yours. I'ma give you ten grand to get yourself started, and I'll see if I can get wit one of my peeps to hook you up wit a legit job."

"Alright," I said, a little relieved.

That was the first time I tried to get out of the "game." I couldn't let myself be consumed by the dark person I was becoming. I had to maintain my balance. Staying "in" wasn't going to help. I was only seventeen and had become part of a violent cycle that seemed never ending. Someone had to end the cycle. Why not me?

Staying out didn't last long, though.

A few months later my life was changed once again with two words. "I'm pregnant."

Paul J. P.

Literacy and Sour Grapes

I was a peasy-head little boy when I first heard the fable about the "Fox and the Sour Grapes." The fox was walking through the woods and came across a bunch of grapes hanging from a vine wrapped around the branch of a tree. He jumped and jumped, trying to reach the grapes, but finally gave up and walked away, saying to himself, "Those grapes were probably sour anyway." Like the fox, I walked away from school and told myself that school knowledge was just a bunch of sour grapes.

I hated getting up in the morning to go to school and sit in boring classes all day. For me, school was just a place I had to go to learn about a lot of things that I would probably never need or use in real life. The truth is that I hated school because I felt that I was too dumb to learn. I could never seem to keep up with the rest of the class in reading, writing, or math. Whenever I went to the teacher's desk to ask about something I was having trouble with, I usually ended up going back to my seat still confused. I eventually stopped asking for help and just sat at my desk and pretended to do the lessons.

I remember how dumb I felt when teachers asked the class to raise our hands to answer questions, and it seemed like half the class always had the answers even before I could figure out what the question was. By the time I was in fifth grade, I found a couple of ways to avoid thinking about how hard it was for me to learn in school. I'd raise my hand in class and ask stupid questions that would make everyone laugh. If we were doing fractions in math class, I'd say things like, "How come they can't just say the number on the top and the number on the bottom, instead of calling them *De-Nom-Ate-Her* and *Num-Ate-Her*?"

I stayed in trouble in school for doing things like banging on my desk like they were drums, talking in class, and fighting boys and girls. After a while, I got used to teachers doing things like making me ball up my fist to whack me on the knuckles with a stack of rulers, giving me spankings on my backside with a thick wooden paddle, or making me stay after school. The one thing teachers would sometimes do that terrified me was have my father come to school and tell him how I had been acting up in class. Daddy would smack the hell out of me or take his belt off and beat me right in front of the class.

Another reason I didn't like school was that I rarely stayed in one school long enough to make any real friends. My father raised me in North Philadelphia along with two brothers and two sisters. We were a poor welfare family, and Daddy constantly moved us from place to place all over North Philly. Sometimes he would take weeks or months for us to be registered in a new school after we moved into a new house or apartment. My most vivid memories of school from the third to sixth grade was how kids viciously teased and called my baby sister and me names. They talked about my clothes that were often old, ripped or stitched up, and sometimes even dirty. They talked about the holes in the bottom of my shoes and how dirty and ugly I was. I became hypersensitive to being teased and often got into trouble for fighting in the schoolyard, and even sometimes in the classroom. I didn't care about getting in trouble for fighting because I learned that being quick to fight was one sure way of stopping other kids from picking on me. Being bullied or becoming a regular victim of cruel and malicious verbal attacks was something that I couldn't accept. Plus, I knew my father would beat me senseless if he ever heard that I let anyone push me around.

I missed even more time from school in junior high than I had in elementary school. Sometimes I didn't go to school because I didn't have money for bus tokens or lunch. I usually played hooky on days we had gym class because I couldn't afford sneakers and gym clothes. By the time I started high school, I had become fully absorbed into the street-gang culture that Philadelphia had become widely known for in the 1960s and '70s. I dropped out of school shortly after I started eleventh grade and devoted most of my time to running the streets, gang warring, getting high, stealing, and robbing.

The streets provided me with something that I never found at home or school. It allowed me to lose myself in a fantasy world where there were no parents, teachers, or other adults controlling and telling me what to do. The streets were full of excitement and adventure, a world wherein no one cared if I could read, spell, write, or do math. In the streets my drinking, fighting, stealing, and willingness to take wild risks gave me power and recognition. I was somebody. I had friends who admired and respected me; enemies who feared and bowed down to me.

Those were my early teen years. As I grew older, I began to discover that the streets had done nothing to prepare me to be a man in the adult world. I didn't have the skills, knowledge, or education to survive or make a future for myself in the real world. Once I applied for a job at a McDonald's fast-food restaurant and didn't get hired because there were ten simple addition and multiplication problems on the application that all had to be answered correctly. I got two answers wrong. That's when I began to realize that everything of value I found in the streets was fake. The streets gave me a false sense of manhood.

All of my gang associates, as well as myself, who quit school to become outlaws and alcoholics suffered "The Peter-Pan Syndrome." We refused to grow up. I was living on animal instincts and driven by selfish desires. I never thought about what I was doing to my life or the lives of my family, friends, and the victims of my crimes. Even more, I was so full of fear, anger, shame, and ignorance that I believed I had no control over my future or the kind of person I could become. I had convinced myself that I could never be smart enough to become anything but a street thug. At age fifteen, I predicted that my ultimate destiny was prison or early death, and I made sure I did everything I could to make that prediction come true.

I was attracted to street-life because I found out that it was a lot easier to get acceptance, recognition, and respect from like-minded peers for doing wrong. I didn't realize that everything I did on the streets was driving me straight to a place where I would be powerless, disrespected, and unrecognized for the rest of my life. But there was always a part of me that wanted to change the direction my life was headed. I went back to school when I was eighteen and, with a lot of hard work, I earned my GED several months after I turned nineteen. However, I waited too long to make up my mind to get out of the street-life. Not even two weeks before my twentieth birthday, I got involved in a street gang homicide and found myself in prison a year later serving a life sentence without the possibility of parole.

It took many years before I began to understand that the reason I couldn't keep up with or learn as fast as other kids in school was not because I was dumb or unable to learn. It was because I missed a lot of school, rarely did homework, and never took learning seriously. I was too filled with shame to ask for help and tried to hide my shame by being rebellious and acting a fool in class. I tried to make up for not being as smart as other kids in school by being tough and slick on the street.

Even after I got my GED, I had doubts about my intelligence. When I came to prison, I decided to continue going to school to prove to myself that I wasn't dumb and discovered that I loved learning. So far, I've been in prison going on thirty years and have earned two college degrees and more than a hundred certificates for my participation in a number of educational programs and other activities.

In 1999, I was blessed with the privilege of assisting a group of outside volunteers who visit the prison on a weekly basis to tutor inmates. I eventually became one of nine inmate tutors in the Graterford Literacy Program. We work with other prisoners who need help with improving their reading, writing and math skills. Being able to help men discover that they have the ability to learn brings so much joy to my heart. Like me, many of them spent years believing that they didn't have what it takes to learn. They had the courage to overcome shame and fear enough to accept help, and—like me—found out that the grapes of knowledge from the learning tree are deliciously sweet.

Suggestions for Writing

1. Choose a time in your life when you made a decision that had negative consequences. Imagine other possible outcomes, and write about it.

2. Write about an experience from the point of view of parents, a person hurt by crime, a police officer, etc.

3. Read "Conspiracy" or "Absence of Light." Have you ever been with a group of friends and done something you didn't want to do because your friends were doing it? Or, have you ever seen your friends do something you weren't okay with when you were with them? Write or tell the story.

4. Read "Welcome to Hell" by Eduardo R. Do you feel that doing time in jail would be easy?

5. What goals do you have for the future? Describe what you hope to accomplish by the time you are 50. Or, write a paragraph for each decade about where you see yourself at age 20, 30, 40, and 50. Or, write about an activity that you used to do that you miss doing. Or, write an essay in which you consider if you are using your time usefully, productively.

6. Read "The Lost Boy." How badly do you crave material possessions: cars, clothes, jewelry, etc.? Or, would you turn to selling drugs if the opportunity were afforded you? Again, do you feel that doing time in jail would be easy? Choose one of these questions, or any combination of them, and discuss them in a short essay.

HOME

Frank R.

HOME

He was an old guy when I met him. I never did know his real name. Had an Indian nickname. Once in a while, I almost come up with it. It wasn't like Brave Warrior or Running Bear. He was called after one of the tribes—like, Apache. It's on the tip of my tongue. He was the only convict who could go and come when he wanted. You might see him anywhere. Him and his baggy pants. Carried an old cloth bag—wide and deep—something like what the fellas used on ice-trucks years ago. The guy had a bit of everything in his cell. If you lost a button, or knob off your TV or radio, he'd find you one. They said he didn't want to go home. Been in prison too long. Some forty years. They said the world had changed too much. I'd heard him say one time, "Go home? This is my home. . ." I don't know if he meant it. He collected stamps. We guys saved them for him. And on a rare occasion—when he wasn't in those baggy pants—he'd hold court on the radiator. Would have his yellowish-gray hair combed to the side. Wore it kind of long. He'd take a puff on his cigar, then smile like he owned the world. I guess a good cigar does that to a fella. When he got sick, he fought to stay out of the hospital. His ankles swelled up so he hardly could walk. The guys would pull him on a wagon to the medication line. He'd wave like an old bear in the circus. The guys kept up a good face. But we felt bad for the old-timer. I was off the cell-block when they carried him out. About a week later we got the news. I still think of that old-timer. But I never did know his real name.

Frank R.

It's This Thing about a Tree

Every once in a while I think about going home. It ain't a day passes that I don't think about it. But every once in a while I think about it like it's really going to happen. When you've been in prison for a long time, you start questioning yourself. You start wondering how you'll act. Being an old-timer myself—most of the things I've known are gone. A guy gotta be a little scared. Will you cry? Keep telling myself that I won't. Ain't cried since I was nine. If I do—where? Will I break down going through the gate? I wouldn't want the hacks to see me. Will it be on the bus? Or on the street? In front of some strangers? Deep inside, I know where. I can't explain it, but I just know. It's this thing about a tree. Guess it must be like that proverbial straw. Can't get it out of my mind. I always see it in my dreams. I'm nearing this tree. I look at it for a while. Walk around it. Then I reach out, holding my breath, and touch it. To see how it feels. I've been waiting to do that all these years. If I ever do—I know I'll cry.

Winfield P.

SANCTUARY

Sanctuary for me is in the midst of a tropical rain forest just after the monsoon rains have washed over every square inch of this lush, green haven. It is so clean and alive. Soft natural sounds of life sing pleasantly in my ears. Flashes of brilliant colors streak across the sunny sky as tropical birds. Enjoying their gift of flight, they spread their wings to catch the cool breeze of the wind, living ships that sail gracefully in our haven. I am happy, safe and at peace in my own garden of Eden in my mind.

Winfield P.
BEAUTY IN THE BEAST

The beast is a huge monster with dimensions that cover sixty-seven acres of land. It is a leviathan of mega tons. The guts are concrete and steel, and could supply enough material to build another Golden Gate Bridge. Encased within the vast maze are tiny honeycomb caves filled with bee-like creatures that race and scurry about the leviathan daily. At the extreme end of this beast, I found myself caught in a wonder of nature that shook my senses. I was inside the chapel behind locked doors. A small window was my only view of freedom. The first thing that captured my attention was snow falling and touching everything and everyone. There were guys in a dog kennel environment attempting to exercise their bodies from long hours of hold time. The snow does not discriminate as man does. As I watched, I saw a side of life that few take note of or know about. I saw two odd shapes moving across the grounds: Canadian geese, just walking like an old married couple on a morning stroll. My mind was boggled and it reeled at the sight of these beautiful, graceful birds, free to be a thousand miles away. Yet there, that day, we were in the same place: a prison. Beauty knows no boundaries, or limits.

Christopher R. W. M.

THE CAGED WINDOW

The glass is too high for me
on tiptoes I see frightened faces

The lucent sun fails to penetrate
the star's luster hidden

Filtered light in the fenced-in pane
the wind sweeps littered streets

Whosh, whosh, whosh
I silently contemplate—

Is it still there
Red bricks walls

The velvet plastic-covered couch
The bronze pheasant wall clock

Will Nanna walk through the door
staggering from a day out shopping

Will anyone appreciate her labor
in the core of her spiritual torment

Is time going by like a scared hare
Or am I too old being born young?"

Elliott E.

DEFINING STORY

One of my best memories starts when I was 10 years old, turning 11. It was the summer of 1995. A man in the neighborhood who was known to sell water-ice, and on occasion puppies, announced that his pit bull was pregnant and would be dropping a litter. I asked him to hold me a puppy. He told me to check with my grandmother and mother. I did so, and convinced the two that the dog belonged to me already. After a while of me bugging them, and telling them I wanted nothing else for my birthday or Christmas but this puppy, they were finally sold on the idea. In October of 1995, the pregnant dog had just delivered two puppies, but one died during birth. I got my puppy the end of October, one month before my 11th birthday. I had the name already picked out for him. As soon as I got him my mom asked me his name. I said Appachie. From the time I got him we did everything together. Appachie walked me to the bus stop in the morning for school. He would even be waiting by the door after school for me. My dog was real protective of me. He wouldn't let just anybody walk up to the two of us without my permission. I learned life lessons from this dog. One lesson was responsibility. It was up to me to provide food for my dog out of my own money. Some people would say that an 11 year old can't even fend for himself, how would he take care of a dog? Well, I solved that problem. I had all the answers—at least I thought so. There was a lady who worked for the city. Still to this day I only know that her job detail is something to do with Fairmount Park. Once a week she would drop off open dog food for the stray dogs in Fairmount Park. My dog and I would come after she had left, and I would collect as much of the food that I could carry. I did this every week until I was told not to bring no more dog food in the house, because the dog has more food than us. I also brought my dog to fist fights that I may have had with others. Other people brought their older brothers and so on. I brought my dog. I knew he would never run on me! I might have got in trouble a few times, because he bit plenty of people, but what can you say, he was protecting me.

I was getting into so much trouble that I had to be sent to live with my father. My dad was afraid of dogs so I couldn't bring Appachie along with me. By this time I was 13 years old, and Appachie was 2 ½. My grandmother wound up selling my dog for crack. I believe once I realized my dog was forever gone, my heart was gone too.

Christopher R. W. M.

BARRICADES

I remember when Papa passed.
Grandma hated life. Papa hated
Grandma and Grandpa. Mamma had
Angie and me out of wedlock.
Brother hated me. I learned to
hate brother. I remember my pain
in hating. It taught me not to
love, not to trust. Brick walls
are to keep positives out—
negatives in. I became a castle of
brick walls, moats, and
drawbridges.

Emotions lay in a heap of decaying
souls. I remember never feeling,
never loving, never touching, never
trying, never trusting, never
opening, never closing, never,
never, never-ever lowering broken
draw bridges. I remember love's
pointed blade, piercing chest,
ribs, heart, soul, spirit, life and
God. I remember darkened crawl
spaces, rats chewing, pets being
swallowed by hungry dogs.

I remember hospitals, needles,
emergency rooms, asthma, heart
pains, growing, withering, seeing

death, remembering life as an
elderly child. I remember being in
my prime at age five—being senile
at age thirteen, being born again
at age nineteen—living, dying,
breathing—waking up from false
stories of "Cat in the Hat,"
"Mickey Mouse Club," and "Captain
Noah."

I remember the metallic taste of
blood—still tasteless to a
tasteful palate. I remember seeing
America for the first time, seeing
liberty chained—seeing monkeys
covering holes in walls, in
society, in prisons, in leaders, in
me, in my family and perpetrating
God. I remember becoming free. I
remember being the slave of Lady
Liberty—her plantation not
residing in New York—but in the
middle of West Philly.

I remember the bombardments of
flaming arrows—from moats, from
drawbridges, and from the clay and
mortar that bonds me to internal and
external prisons. I remember seeing
my face on other living beings, even
on the hungered snouts of beasts. I
remember crying—I remember dying.

I remember not feeling, never loving,
never trusting, never being free, and

never allowing humanity in the
demolished cell I refer to as my
human vessel. I remember wood chips
from doors, lacerated faces, blood
red eyes filled with anger, hate,
revenge, malice, and brimmed over
with maddened tears. I remember
water—mixed with life-giving blood,
running over bathtubs—tears mingled
with iodine and ivory soap.

I remember life and death courting,
giggling on my front porch, creeping
through the front door making
shushing sounds. I remember letting
go of the ropes that connected me to
humanity. I remember tumbling,
flailing and grasping for ghosts that
once walked the earth as blind and
deaf elders. I always remember.

Winfield P.

I CAN SOAR

Wow—After two decades and a half, the big gate is open to me. It is a true major event—I am free—No longer bound by the physical limits of my once concrete prison—I am in awe—as the true depth of this life change washes over each fiber of my being—saturating my senses with a mixture of emotions and feelings that goes from anxiety, elation, fear, joy, panic. All because I am about to step beyond the threshold of incarceration into the free world and a universe of human experience and growth that can never be realized in jail.

For some reason I am aware of the air. It is different outside of prison. The air is full of smells and taste—aromas and fragrance long forgotten but today very familiar—life everywhere, even in the loud noise of living, I can feel and hear it. Now I move eagerly into the vast future that lies ahead one step at a time, into the unknown. The people who came to get me, family and friend, think that I am a bit weird as there is no haste and urgency on my part to get in the car. To me at this moment it is an overcrowded cell that is mobile—I again experience a sense of discomfort and panic as thoughts of riding in this car, a station wagon, - Country Squire reminds me that I have not been in a car for over twenty-five years. Motion sickness. Will I throw up? How embarrassing. Will I stand here forever, smile. So why is my Father speeding? Does he feel a sense of excitement and joy about my release today? That makes a lot of sense as he and the entire family as well as friends are affected and touched by my coming home today—but I don't think we need to do it via the Indy Speedway. Everything is flying past my eyes in a blur—I hear this sound that only happens when a car is in motion—Oh man it is me—my father is driving at the speed limit—I still have the jail lifestyle with me so my perception is off. What was normal does not apply out here in the real world. I wonder if I will ever grow out of this experience and lose all of the deep inner hidden scars and misery of jailhouse life—God I hope so.

There is a steady chant of conversation in the car about my well-being and what I have in mind to do now that I am free. It is hard to plan and think past this car ride. I hear somebody say, "We are going to party hard." I respond with, "That will have to wait until later." Right now, take me to the State building so that I can register with my parole officer—collect some money, and of course, get the rules of conduct down while I am here—then I stop at a nice greasy family restaurant. That will be my lunch—fried chicken, shrimp, biscuits, French fries, lemon cream pie and a quart of orange juice. AHA—no guards—just me and my first meal out of jail. It is delicious for real. Now to the house I will be staying in for a while. Well, actually my room—Funny, I still want to decorate it like my old cell. This room is big and comfortable. I can really relax in here, plus, no locks on the doors. Well, now to change my clothes for the home-coming party. So many choices of colors and textures. No more browns with D.O.C. on the back. I like jeans—pullover sweatshirt, light blue—A pair of mountain boots, dark brown, and a dungaree jacket. Now to mingle and socialize with the family and friends. Also meet some new people but mainly enjoy myself under free conditions.

The food at the party was great. I stuffed myself because there were so many delicious treats I had not tasted in years. Now I am on a natural high, intoxicated by the pure goodness of freedom. Seen most of the family, reestablished the bonds of friendship. It is night and I can actually see the moon and stars again—a perfect end to one of the best days of my life. Now to sleep in a real bed—No guards with flashlights shining in my face to see if I am alive. Tonight I shall sleep peacefully for the first time in twenty-five years. Tonight there is no care or concerns to worry about. I shall dream again. But tonight this dream will be about me being free—successfully accomplishing all my desires and goals. I can soar because I am free … .

Suggestions for Writing

1. Describe a place where you can go for safety. It can be a place that makes you feel physically safe, or it can be a place in your mind that makes you feel safe.

2. Write a response to the poem, "Barricades." When something goes wrong, do you talk to people, or do you put up walls and deal with everything on your own? Which do you think is better to do? Why?

3. Read "Sanctuary." Are there any places in the world that you would like to see? Why would you like to go there?

4. Read "Beauty in the Beast." Is there anything beautiful in your life? Describe it. Or, describe a special friend that you enjoy being with?

5. Read "I Can Soar." Can you imagine not being able to come and go as you please? Or, how can you protect your freedoms so that you can enjoy them forever? Write a short piece in which you answer one or both of these questions.

FAMILY

Paul J. P.

Eyes Like My Father

It's January 20, 2007...

A Polaroid snapshot of a wheelchair-bound father visiting his son in prison might give one pause to recall the old adage, "A picture is worth a thousand words." Looking at this photo of me and my father, I think of the thousand unspoken words locked inside my heart.

We pose side by side smiling for the camera. Dressed in a nicely pressed dark grey outfit with a white towel covering his shoulders, Daddy leans forward in his wheelchair with elbows resting on widespread knees.

I've often heard women talk sarcastically about how a son of theirs had many of the same character traits of his father. They'd say things like, "That damn boy is just like his Daddy!" I don't know if, or to what extent, a child can genetically inherit personality, posture, or temperament from a parent, but I've known a few guys with sons that look, walk, talk, and act just like them. I'm talking about guys who have been incarcerated and had little or no contact with their children while they were growing up. That has always made me wonder how much, if any, of Daddy's character I inherited genetically, as opposed to assimilated while he was raising me.

The most striking thing about Daddy in this picture is probably the image of his deformed hands clasped together like a pile of dry kindling. With crooked fingers that twisted and curved because of webbed skin that prevented them from being fully extended, those intimidating hands could frighten an infant or repulse even an undertaker. With huge bulging knuckles, those mutilated hands could transform into stone fists. He claims a grenade exploded in his hands when he was in the army.

I've known those hands all my life, strong hands that picked me up as a child, threw me in the air and caught me in play, hands that fed and protected our family through a life of hard times. Those hands could fix broken plumbing, doors, old TVs, cars, you name it. But they were also hands that smacked, punched, and beat Mommy in drunken fits of anger, hands that fought, stabbed, or shot any man or woman unfortunate enough to awaken their violent wrath.

The balding old-timer in this photo is but an echo of the man that had such a dark impact on my youth. Afflicted with Alzheimer's, arthritis, and an assortment of other ailments, he gazes square shouldered into the camera. A closed, toothless-mouth smile conveys the self-assured confidence of a man who sees himself as having been endowed with photogenic features. The strong, solid physique of a young cruiserweight boxer that once stood tall and erect in the face of any adverse situation has been reduced to a flimsy coat hanger. But the flame of an indomitable spirit still burns deep within his eyes.

Dressed in a dark brown prison jumpsuit that matches a kidney bean complexion, I'm squatted on my left knee next to his wheelchair. My left arm rests on the back of the chair with right forearm relaxing on my right bended knee. A fat-cheeked smile revealing the upper row of my teeth gives the impression of a "*Kodak Moment*" between father and son.

An almost life-size mural in the background imbues the photo with a familial atmosphere. A serene outdoor setting filled with several shades of blue sky and silhouettes of trees with naked branches depicts a young mother playing with her child. The child appears to be climbing a white pole. Only its ankles and little white and blue, low-top, sneakers are visible. Wrapped in a white terrycloth bathrobe, the mother stands next to the pole. Her left arm is slightly raised and extended as if poised to catch the child in the event it should fall. With honey-colored skin and a Dentine smile, her head is turned facing the camera, looking as if she's aware that she is part of our photo.

A surge of nostalgic warmth permeates my body as I reflect on this deceptively congenial snapshot. I remember how, as a little boy, whenever Daddy walked into the house I'd jump up and down shouting "Daddy's home, Daddy's home!" Filled with the joy of love for the coolest Daddy in the world, I'd run and jump into his arms. My two younger brothers and I often mimicked the long strides of his crazy cool stroll and his well practiced use of profanity.

Yeah, in those days Daddy was my hero. With only a third grade education, he was an amazingly resourceful and quick witted lady's man, who could charm a witch out of her broom. "I'm a man amongst men," he sometimes roared while talking trash and swapping war stories with some of his drinking buddies. I can still picture him bragging about having fathered thirty kids by a multitude of women. I imagine that if we ever had a family reunion it would be likened to a poverty convention— speaker after speaker would give testimony to horror stories of a life of hardship and Daddy's proclivity for verbal and physical assault, while at the same time professing their love for a father who possessed the charisma and hypnotic charm of a master pimp.

Can't say exactly when it started, but in my early adolescence the construction of an invisible emotional wall between us began that had since become thicker and higher than the forty foot wall surrounding this purgatory called prison that I've been trapped in for the past three and a half decades. In between the raging storms of whippings and criticism from early adolescence until my mid teens, I can recall no tender father and son moments when I was praised for something I had achieved or done well.

Prior to my being confiscated like black contraband by the criminal justice system, Daddy and I did forge a sort of unholy bond. In this photo there is only a marginal resemblance of father and son around the eyes and forehead. But in my teens I had embraced the lifestyle of a street gang warrior and developed a mentality and character almost identical to his. Even though he never failed to punish or admonish me whenever I got into trouble with the law, my self-willed stubbornness and indulgence in a level of crime and violence that surpassed his own seemed to impress him. During my short-lived criminal career, he and I occasionally bonded as partners in crime, especially when he needed backup when outnumbered in potential physical confrontations. But the emotional wall between us always remained intact.

You see, Daddy was ultra old-school, forged in the triple threat furnace of poverty, racial oppression, and lack of education. Raised in an era where hyper-masculinity was the prevailing concept of manhood in many black communities, overt displays of pain, remorse, or compassionate sentiment were viewed as signs of weakness.

I often wondered if the reason he was so hard on me as a child was because he saw that I had a sensitive nature and just couldn't reconcile that aspect of my character with his idea of manhood. In my teens I had neutralized my capacity to feel compassion by sedating it with alcohol. I armor-plated my heart with a do-or-die street warrior philosophy that gave free reign to anger and ego massaging pleasures as a means to compensate for a host of insecurities.

Prison or death was the inevitable end to the path of self-destruction I had eagerly followed in my youth. Daddy would have disowned me if he ever knew how many nights I lay curled up on my cell bunk in a fetal position, weeping while contemplating escape through death. He would have spit in my face and called me a pussy if he saw how my naked soul shamelessly wallowed in a puddle of self-pity as walls of doubt closed in like a garbage compressor fusing memories of bad choices into a compact block of raw sewage.

While trembling in the dark, cold depths of despair, I could hear Daddy's bulldoggish voice barking at me: "Git cho ass up and act like a fuckin' man!" I can't say precisely when it happened, or even what it was, but something deeply profound was triggered inside me. I'm not talking about divine revelation or religious conversion. It was more like something on a cellular level, a visceral message from my innermost being that said, "Let it happen."

I allowed the stormy sea of emotions I had been struggling against most of my life to rise up and swallow me whole. As I sank into the belly of my soul, I saw the shattered remains of painful memories stuck in the mud of regret like old sunken shipwrecks at the bottom of the sea. Then, I felt as though I'd been pulled into a powerful undercurrent that dragged me at the speed of thought far into my past. I saw the lost little boy that was me and discovered a truth that had eluded me for years. The moment of clarity smacked me back into reality. Emotionally, I had been living my life like I was still that love-starved little boy, seeking acceptance and approval from a parent whose social orientation made him incapable of expressing the kind of nurturing affection a healthy child needs.

I had unknowingly grown up suppressing my innate sense of humanity in order to conform to my father's and street gang associates' concept of manhood. That awakening was the genesis of a seismic shift in the way I viewed the world and, more importantly, myself. I turned my prison cell into a cocoon where I began the painful process of self transformation that enabled me to accomplish things that I never would have imagined when I was in my teens. I read books on music, art, philosophy, psychology, sociology, religions, and science—acquiring a thirst for knowledge that empowered me with a sense of purpose and the tools to make positive contributions to the lives of those around me.

I still have unresolved issues and character flaws that need to be addressed. Some emotional wounds from my past are still in the process of healing. But I've won a hard fought victory against the shortsighted, life-negating part of my spirit. I've managed to reverse polarity to the life-affirming part of the spirit within that gives each of us the capacity to feel compassion, have empathy, employ reason and exercise self-control.

Although the me squatting next to my father in this photo has long since become a self-defined, independent-thinking man, there are a number of positive character traits I modeled from him that I've retained and will be forever grateful for. I've long ago forgiven him for whatever role he may have played in my becoming a crime- and violence-prone youth. But more importantly, I've forgiven myself. Not knowing that the day we took this picture would be the last time I'd ever see him, my only regret is that I never told him how I feel. He passed away seven months after this visit, July 24, 2007. But even without having heard the words, I knew in the end he was proud of the man I had become. As for love, that's something he was always able to see in my eyes as clearly as he saw the hate.

Ronald J. C.

LEONA'S GIFT

My most cherished Christmas gift was a pair of shoes bought for me by Joey's mother, Ms. Leona, a woman who looked like the actress Sophia Loren. She was tall, with dark long flowing hair that fell to her shoulders like a veil. She had an olive complexion and cameo face. Often with a smile and an open heart, she was pleasant to look at and comforting to be with. She was forty five, and I fourteen.

I met Ms. Leona mid-summer 1959, when I was fifteen years old, through her son Joey, whom I met soon after running away from a foster home. I was living on the streets of downtown Philadelphia. Often begging and stealing for food, sleeping in all night movie houses, at times in back of abandoned cars parked in darkened lots. Telling Joey this soon after we met, he invited me to come home with him. His mother, Ms. Leona, was very receptive of me. With her Mediterranean look, she looked like the mother I always imagined mine to be. She acted as if she were. She opened a folding bed for me to sleep on that night, asked her son to give me clean clothes, and urged me to eat as much as I could. Such treatment! I assumed Joey told his mother of my predicament. He did. For within that day she knew why I had nowhere to go. I felt anxious about her knowing my secret; however, rather than call the police or Child-Welfare Service, she was emphatic about me living with them.

They lived on the sixteenth floor, in the Rittenhouse Towers, which overlooked Center City. Other than Joey and his mother, his younger sister Donna and the housekeeper, Ms. Morrella, lived in the highrise apartment. One that had three bedrooms, a large living room, bathroom, and kitchen, with a patio to enjoy the view. For a scroungy runaway kid looking for shelter, what a way to live! In some uncanny and immediate way, I now had a brother close in age to hang out with, a sister, fun to be with, someone's mother caring for me, and a housekeeper who cooked our meals. No longer hungry, with a roof over my head, I had it made.

In short time, so settled was I that one day I saw Joey's mom semi-undressed. She had on black panties and a white bra, which I took in stride. What was shocking, she had a wooden leg. Seeing me stare at it, she looked at me for a moment, gave me a smile, then went about dressing for work. She was a nightclub singer. Each evening, except for Sundays, she would dress up like a beauty queen. Rhinestone gowns, chiffon dresses, silky scarfs and Easter-like hats she wore to work. In the wee hours of the morning she would return home, alone. Then, to my surprise, one early morning, an elderly man dressed in a suit walked into the apartment with Ms. Leona. He casually introduced himself as Mr. Brown, a friend of the family.

Within a week after meeting him, Joey's mom was telling me we were moving out of the apartment. Mr. Brown was a railroad executive who lived in the countryside, and we were moving in with him. I never imagined we would be moving into such a house as he owned. Tudor-style, with its multiple gables, stained glass windows, crafted doors, thick wide beams of dark lumber stretched across high ceilings of large white rooms, Persian rugs atop parquet floors, brocaded furniture, Tiffany lamps, textured quilts and comfortable beds. The land, like a golf course around it, large as a football field, a lake to one side and trees like cathedrals to the other.

While Joey and Donna were at school, I fell into a routine of visiting the ducks on the lake, playing in the woods, doing chores, watching TV, going weekly to the mall with Ms. Leona, and eating like the son of a squire. Days passed into months. Before I knew it, it was Christmas Eve.

Early that day, Joey's grandfather came to pick up him and his sister. Mr. Brown was at work, and Ms. Morrella, the housekeeper, was cooking turkey. It was then that Ms. Leona asked me if I wanted to go shopping with her. She needed to pick up a few things and was on her way to the city. Eagerly, I replied yes, of course. Quickly dressed, I found myself shoveling snow off the hood and windshield of the car, clearing the driveway and tires of snow. Finally, off we drove.

Sitting in the front seat looking at Ms. Leona, I thought how fortunate it was that her left leg was wood rather than her right.

Otherwise, it would be quite hard to drive. The radio in the car was on, and it was warm inside. Telephone poles, silos, farmhouses, dots of horses, a few cows here and there, snow-covered pine trees and rolling hillsides passed my eyes like postcards. Without worry and feeling protected, I was at peace with the world.

As if in tune with my state of mind, in a soft voice, I heard, "Ronald, I want to adopt you. What do you think of the idea?" Startled by her question, I didn't know what to say. Seeing my bewildered look, Ms. Leona, reaching with her right hand, lovingly shuffled the hair on my head. Then with a smile, she said, "I can't bear to see you living back on the streets." Looking at her as she spoke, with her warm disarming brown eyes, I felt a lava of love for her at that moment, as any son could have for his mother.

Moments of silence passed between us. I then asked, "Will they have to take me back in custody for this to happen?"

"Honestly, I don't know, Ronald, but I'll try my best to keep you with me. Something has to be done. You can't miss another year of school, and to register you in it, I must have your birth certificate and papers affirming that I am your legal guardian."

"Will that mean, Ms. Leona, that Mr. Brown will become my step-father?"

"Not necessarily, Ronald," she replied, "only if I marry him. I have known him for fifteen years. He's twice proposed to me, and I am not getting any younger. He's as kind and loving as my first husband, Gerald, was. Ronald, what do you think of him?"

"Though he's not often around because of work, I like him, Ms. Leona. He's never hit or scolded me as other foster parents have. He's also funny in his own way, and I like the aroma from the pipe he smokes."

"Ronald, I know you're guarded about your parents, but what happened to them? Did they die and that's why you were placed in foster homes?

"I really don't know, Ms. Leona; all I know, as far back as I can remember, I've been in foster homes. The ones I liked, I was taken from. Others I ran away."

"Well, Ronald, hopefully you won't run away from us. That would break my heart."

"No, Ms. Leona, I would never do that. You're one of the nicest persons I know."

"Good, now on a happier note, what do you think of Christmas?"

"I like many things about Christmas, Ms. Leona. The gifts people give and the parties they have. Also, I like how the lights look that Joey and I helped put on the house, the decorated tree in the living room, and the turkey Ms. Morrella was cooking, and I like the pies she's already made." As I said that we went from countryside to Center City, pulling into a parking space on South Street. At the age of fourteen, as I remember, a winter wonderland of a street to behold. Green, red, and gold garland and multiple strings of colored lights were strung high across the full length of South Street and beyond. Snow descended gently to the ground. A short old man in the middle of the block wearing a longshoreman's hat and pea coat, stood at his cart with steam coming out of his mouth, and barked, "Hot walnuts! Hot walnuts! Get them while they're hot!" The aroma of walnuts roasting on hot coals oozed from the old man's cart and teased my nostrils.

Taking it all in, there was a Santa Claus with a silver bell in his hand, ringing in the season. Salvation Army singing Silent Night. There were throngs of people, some walking, others in a rush, and many gazing in shop windows. Boxes of chocolates, cookies, candies, pies and cakes of every kind on dazzling display. Next door, electric trains, bikes, scooters, bats, hats and gloves, action toys and G.I. Joe's all bidding for attention. Such it was with the different colored cheeses and delicious looking meats hanging from stainless steel hooks.

At the dress shop we stopped. Manikins in the window dressed like starlets got Ms. Leona's attention. "Ronald, go to the corner store and pick out yourself a pair of shoes, I'll be there shortly."

Doing as she asked, to my surprise, Florsheim, a men's store, was there. As I walked in, a young man wearing a white shirt and dark tie approached and asked if he could be of help. I felt awkward not having Ms. Leona with me, so I told the salesman what Ms. Leona told me to do, and as an afterthought mentioned her name.

"Come with me," he said, "I know her." Now relaxed and inhaling the scent of new leather and men's cologne, I was escorted to the rear of the store. "Have anything in mind?" he asked before I sat down.

"Not really, sir" I replied.

"Call me Ted," he said. "By the way, what size shoe do you wear?"

"Size eight, sir, I mean, Mr. Ted."

Within moments he had a white shoe box in his hand and five other shoe boxes sitting on the table. "What do you think?" Ted said, as he pulled the shoes from the box and showed them to me. Any new pair of shoes looked good to me. "I like them, Ted," I replied.

"Try them on, and before we decide, I have others you may also like." Taking off my shoes I worried my socks may stink. That thought seemed always to occur when the nuns of the Catholic Child Services had me try on shoes. Shoes routinely provided to foster parents for me. Though the shoes fit, they seemed stiff, and if my memory serves me correctly, my socks didn't stink.

"Ted, may I try on another pair?" Quickly he had them in his hands. This pair had no shoe strings, but tassels. I thought they looked neat. Walking back and forth in them I thought to myself, these shoes look pretty expensive. It was then I heard Ms. Leona's voice. "How's my soldier making out?"

Both Ted and I turned to see Ms. Leona with a smile on her face and two gift-wrapped boxes under her arms. "I like the shoes, Ronald," she told me. "What do you think?"

"Me, too," I said.

I liked them so much I didn't want to take them off, but I did when I heard Ms. Leona tell Ted, "Please wrap them, these shoes are going under our tree."

While I pulled on my old shoes, Ted went to the back store room and returned with two gift-wrapped shoe boxes. Handing one to me, the other to Ms. Leona, I heard him ask her, "How's Joey?"

"He's with his grandparents," Ms. Leona replied. "I'll tell Joey you were asking for him. And let's hope he likes his shoes."

"Merry Christmas, Leona, and drive carefully," Ted said, as we exited the store. Ms. Leona turned and thanked Ted for everything, and wished him and his family a Merry Christmas.

As we walked through the snow back to the car with my new shoes tucked under my arm, I asked Ms. Leona, "Can I help with the boxes?"

"Thanks, Ronald." Handing two of them to me, she hurried to the car and opened the door. I put the gift boxes in the back seat and then cleared the windshield of snow.

We pulled out of our parking space. The Christmas lights strung across South Street seemed brighter. Shortly afterwards, when reaching the expressway, Ms. Leona asked, "Are you happy, son?" Her emphasis on son caught me off guard. Sort of choked up, I blurted out, "Very much, Mom."

"No. Ms. Leona" she said. Slowing the car to almost a stop, she leaned over and kissed me on my cheek. I turned my face to hide my tears.

Winfield P.

I Saw My Friend Again

Over the years, I have met many people. Some have been able to breach the tough shell of my heart and become a precious gem. A jewel of shared experiences, memories, and time. A jewel that I actually miss when their beautiful presence is not around. Why is it so significant when I see this friend again? Is it realizing that the bonds of friendship are so strong, that they transcend the walls of a prison? I am very glad and happy to see my friend again alive, strong, and filled with the vibrant fire of life.

James T.

ENCOUNTERS WITH FATHERHOOD

The group sessions I attend three times a week in the Deputy's Complex consist of a mix of 18 men, black, white and Hispanic, ranging in age between 21 and 70 with varying attitudes and opinions on a variety of subjects.

This day the inmate facilitator, addressing the issue of fatherhood, asked the group, "What would your school age children say when asked by the teacher what their father's occupation was?"

As prisoners and absent fathers from our children's lives, the question caught us all off guard. The question registered the thought in my mind that if we really loved our children as much as we claimed, then what were we doing in prison? And what's more, what would be our intentions with our children upon release? That's just the way I took it, mainly because it had been true in my case. Prison has a way of bringing out the best of intentions in fathers with respect to their children. Like some of these guys, I'd been released before as a young man with love in my heart for my sons, yet had been guilty of the neglect implied. I imagine many of us in the room felt as I did to one degree or another.

Everyone looked around the room at each other with a sense of embarrassment and guilt, waiting to see who would answer first. In my mind, it wasn't that many of us in the room hadn't had jobs before. The implied meaning I felt by the question was the responsibility of providing for our children as a father from that job, which I suspect was not the case in most instances.

I remember being asked what my parents' occupations were in open class. I was in the sixth grade. My parents were hard working people, but I felt a sense of shame in saying in open class that my mother worked as a cleaning woman for the British Embassy and that my father worked as a laborer for the electric company. That being the case, I wondered how my sons felt about me and what answer they gave as my employment as someone who was an absent father from their lives. No, I wanted to be a good father. But the truth of the matter was that I was not. The reality is that because of the risky lifestyle I lived, my sons were better off without me, even knowing that I resented the idea of another man marrying my ex-wife and being the father to my sons that I should have been. Yet the fact remains that my sons turned out okay with another man in the role of stepfather.

Anyway, no one in the group answered the question about what their children would say about their father's employment. Was the question intended to be answered, or raised just to make a point? But if that question was difficult, then I'd say the next one was a dagger in the heart of a father's responsibility towards his children when the facilitator asked, "How many of you have attended a PTA meeting with your children?"

In other sessions we'd talk about "manhood" and how, even in our criminal lifestyle, we managed to provide "material" things for our children. But this question was an indictment of the real concern we held for our children.

As a child, I lived a half block from Mott School. PTA meetings were held in the school auditorium at night, so I got a chance to see how many parents attended. I felt bad that my parents never attended. I was a failing student and remember specific requests by the teacher for my parents to attend those sessions to discuss my behavior and grades in particular. I told my mother this, but she worked nights and couldn't make it. My father was never considered. Today, I can only imagine how many minority school-age children of incarcerated parents are affected in this way by the large number of black men represented in prisons across this nation.

My sense was that a father was a man his children run to greet when he comes home from work. It wasn't like that with me. Much of the time I spent avoiding my father for fear of being spoken harshly to and having my feelings hurt.

I used to like visiting my oldest sister Shirley's house because of the way her husband showed affection for his children. I wished my father would relate to me like that.

I never stopped looking for a father figure in my life. A father teaches and corrects the perception in a child when he goes wrong. Tack Ross served as a father figure to me in prison as a young man. He taught me things about life. I asked questions that he gave helpful answers to.

Years later, I witnessed another situation in prison that points to the importance of fatherhood. To protect the identity of the father in question, I'll just say his name was Ali. He was a lifer and a very good friend. Ali's young son is the person I'm talking about. He was around 19 or 20 years old and looked just like his father. I don't know what was going on in his life on the outside, but it seemed he had a need of actually being with his father, even if it meant coming to prison to serve time.

Ali's son never had much time. And of all the prisons in the state, he always managed to get to Graterford and live on the same block as his father. They were constant companions for the six to nine months his son would be here. Even when Ali was at work, his son was in his cell watching TV, waiting for him to return. Ali was a wise father, and I know he was feeding his son whatever it was he needed from him. I saw admiration and contentment on that young man's face when he was with his father. Twice I saw Ali's son come in Graterford to be with his father like that. Ali died years ago and his son has not returned to prison since.

I've witnessed many father-son relationships here in Graterford. To me, it is an indication of fathers failing their sons as I have. On the other hand, like Tack Ross, I've been regarded as a father figure to some of the young men here. I give them the benefit of what I know. Of what I missed and wished I'd had from my father.

For some reason my ex-wife, Viola, made sure our sons remained in my life in spite of my imprisonment up here in Pennsylvania. I called and talked with them on a regular basis. When the boys were about 9 and 10 years old, she would let them come to Philadelphia and stay with friends of mine who brought them to the prison for visits two or three times a year. I once remember asking Viola why she allowed the boys to remain in my life in face of all the changes I'd taken her through. She said, "So that one day you could make them proud of you."

Deserving nothing from her, it is for that reason I could never stop loving her in my heart and soul. I look at life from this place at times hoping for an opportunity to talk with her just as badly as I want my freedom. It is important for me to let her know how much I've always appreciated her and want to apologize to her for letting a good woman down.

I had another son out of wedlock – David. I hadn't heard from his mother for many years. She gave birth to David in 1961. Marcus and Orlando had heard about this half brother of theirs, but never met him even though they live close by in Washington, DC. And it was in the early 1980s that Mary Beavers, David's mother, found out where I was through my mother. Mary wanted David to know his father and made it happen.

When my sons came of age and were married with families of their own, the three of them got together and came to see me. When I learned of this I was happy about it, but at the same time, was unsure of how the visit would go. What had their mothers told them about me? What did they feel about me? What did they want to know? What would I say to them? All these questions ran through my mind.

On the day of the visit, I opened myself up to them, letting them know they could ask me anything they liked. It was on a Sunday, a day when the visitor's room was most crowded. Back then, the visitor's room was more visitor-friendly in that the chairs could be arranged in a tight circle where we could face each other, not like they are now on an immoveable straight line, making it hard to talk to more than one person at a time. David, being the tallest of us, got his height from his mother. One could see he was a Taylor in all other respects as far as looks went. As it turned out, it was a visit where we got a chance to share many experiences with one another. Marcus had gone into the Navy, came out and got married. Orlando finished school, got a good job and got married. David had more of an experience like mine in that for a period of time, he ran the streets selling drugs, drinking and living a risky lifestyle until he woke up and turned his life around after being busted. He said, "The thought of doing the same thing to my children that my father had done to me was the thing that turned my life around in that jail cell."

136

Each of them wanted me to meet their wives and children. They wanted my grandchildren to know me. Since that visit, the relationship with my sons has remained strong.

I was fortunate enough to win a new trial and make bail on this case in 1977. While out on bail, I visited my parents' home in DC. Everybody was glad to see me. But if my father was the same, I expected some kind of criticism or admonishment from him. At one point during the evening, he came downstairs to the living room and told me to come upstairs. He wanted to talk to me alone. In his bedroom, he sat down on his bed and took my hand, guiding me to sit right down next to him. My father turned to me and asked, "Did you do that?" Meaning did I kill someone. That was to be decided in court, so for the sake of my father, I said, "No."

Then my father did something I never expected. He never showed tender affection for me. He took out his wallet and gave me a twenty dollar bill. I knew what it meant. And when we stood, he embraced me for the first time in my life. Tears came to my eyes, and I knew that this man that I thought didn't care that much for me, loved me all along. I left that room knowing that I would cherish that moment for the rest of my life.

I folded that twenty-dollar bill and placed it in a separate slot in my wallet. When I got back to Philly, it was out of respect for my father as a working man that I went to a Thrift Shop and bought a used jumpsuit to work in on my job at the gas station.

My sons are well aware of the work I do with the men in this prison to help guide their lives on the right path. On February 11, 1998, a young man I'd befriended over the years dropped a note in my cell on the morning of his release expressing the value of my relationship to him. In it he wrote, "My dear brother, my friend, mentor and also in many ways, my father figure, I know that Allah forbids us to call those who are not our fathers that, but he also knows that this is the description that can best describe the love I have in my heart for you. I wonder if your boys really know how much has been taken from them and what a wonderful dad they really, really have."

I call my sons long distance once a month. Recently, when talking to my oldest son, Marcus, I asked about his teenage son. I picked up from him that some things were going on with his son, but he was reluctant to suggest he might need some outside help. He had already told me enough in previous conversations for me to know what the concerns were. My instincts came into play. I didn't press it. Instead, recently when I called, I made sure I spoke with Marcus, his wife and my grandson, which was their only child. I told him I would write to him. He said he'd like that and would write back.

I recently received my first letter from him. In response to a comment he made about where his head was at seventeen, I wrote, "Man...I'm thinking back to where my head was at 17. My priorities were very confused at the time. My current situation in life can be traced back to that period. What I needed back then was a mentor to help me understand a lot of stuff I was dealing with. I was not close with my father, even though I grew up in his house, under his care. Hindsight is 20/20 vision. My father was a good man and I totally missed the cues he offered for me to interact with him and the chance to know him better, to learn from him."

I told my grandson, "I am feeling some deep stuff for you. I want you to know me."

No one in the family knows me....really. I seem to be appreciated by the younger men I interact with here and it is natural that I'd want to benefit my own blood. That is why I told him I want him to visit me alone.

The last time I called, his father said, "Your grandson told me you wanted him to come see you. Thanks, Dad."

Suggestions for Writing

1. Explain the importance of family in your life.

2. Tell a story of a time when a family member or a friend helped you make an important decision.

3. Can good friends be like family?

4. Read "A Mother's Touch" in the Letters section and "Eyes Like My Father" in the family section. What qualities make for a good parent? Or, how are you like your mother or father in a good way? A bad way?

5. Read "Leona's Gift." Why did Ronald cry when he called Ms. Leona, Mom? Why did Ronald turn his face from her when he cried in the car?

A CONVERSATION
WITH A POET

For this section of the book, the men were invited to write creative responses to four poems: Charles Simic's "Two Dogs," Jared Carter's "The Purpose of Poetry," William Stafford's "Traveling through the Dark," and Etheridge Knight's "Belly Song."

Permissions were secured to reprint the former three, but with the latter, the editors and publishers were unable to ascertain or get in touch with the copyright holder. Because Mr. Knight died some years ago, we did not want to publish the poem without the respect of having secured a permission. However, the poem can be accessed on-line, and we invited all readers who wish to read it to do so.

We thank the first three poets we were able to get in touch with for kind and generous permission to reprint their poems.

—The editors and publishers

Charles Simic

Born in 1938 in Belgrade, Charles Simic lives in New Hamshire, where he is a professor of literature at the University of New Hampshire. He has published many books of poetry and prose and won many prizes, including the Pulitzer Prize for poetry.

Jared Carter

Jared Carter's most recent book is *Darkened Rooms of Summer: New and Selected Poems*, published by the University of Nebraska Press. He lives in Indiana.

William Stafford

William Stafford (1914-1993) was an American poet and pacifist. In 1970 he was appointed Consultant in Poetry to the Library of Congress (the former title of the U.S. Poet Laureate). His first collection of poetry, *Traveling Through the Dark*, published when he was forty-eight years old, won the National Book Award for poetry in 1963. He went on to write and publish many books of poetry, prose and translations.

Charles Simic

TWO DOGS

For Charles and Holly

An old dog afraid of his own shadow
In some Southern town.
The story told me by a woman going blind,
One fine summer evening
As shadows were creeping
Out of the New Hampshire woods,
A long street with just a worried dog
And a couple of dusty chickens,
And all that sun beating down
In that nameless Southern town.

It made me remember the Germans marching
Past our house in 1944.
The way everybody stood on the sidewalk
Watching them out of the corner of the eye,
The earth trembling, death going by . . .
A little dog ran into the street
And got entangled with the soldiers' feet.
A kick made him fly as if he had wings.
That's what I keep seeing!
Night coming down. A dog with wings.

Jared Carter

THE PURPOSE OF POETRY

This old man grazed thirty head of cattle
in a valley just north of the covered bridge
on the Mississinewa, where the reservoir
stands today. Had a black border collie
and a half-breed sheep dog with one eye.
The dogs took the cows to pasture each morning
and brought them home again at night
and herded them into the barn. The old man
would slip a wooden bar across both doors.
One dog slept on the front porch, one on the back.

He was waiting there one evening
listening to the animals coming home
when a man from the courthouse stopped
to tell him how the new reservoir
was going to flood all his property.
They both knew he was too far up in years
to farm anywhere else. He had a daughter
who lived in Florida, in a trailer park.
He should sell now and go stay with her.
The man helped bar the doors before he left.

He had only known dirt under his fingernails
and trips to town on Saturday mornings
since he was a boy. Always he had been around
cattle, and trees, and land near the river.
Evenings by the barn he could hear the dogs
talking to each other as they brought in
the herd; and the cows answering them.

It was the clearest thing he knew. That night
He shot both dogs and then himself.
The purpose of poetry is to tell us about life.

William Stafford

TRAVELING THROUGH THE DARK

Traveling through the dark I found a deer
dead on the edge of the Wilson River road.
It is usually best to roll them into the canyon:
that road is narrow; to swerve might make more dead.

By glow of the tail-light I stumbled back of the car
and stood by the heap, a doe, a recent killing;
she had stiffened already, almost cold.
I dragged her off; she was large in the belly.

My fingers touching her side brought me the reason—
her side was warm; her fawn lay there waiting,
alive, still, never to be born.
Beside that mountain road I hesitated.

The car aimed ahead its lowered parking lights;
under the hood purred the steady engine.
I stood in the glare of the warm exhaust turning red;
around our group I could hear the wilderness listen.

I thought hard for us all—my only swerving—,
then pushed her over the edge into the river.

Creative Responses

A poem written in response to Charles Simic's "Two Dogs"

James T.

AN AMERICAN ALLEGORY

Recall, the generations of human degradation
in the south-lands of America,
the vicious atrocities heaped upon the defenseless,
loyal Black Slave…citizens
beaten into submission in the name of Democracy.
The story told by the lady in the Harbor,
chained at the foot going blind to justice
with all that light of truth beating down.
John Brown creeping out of the shadows
from New Hampshire to Virginia
striking a blow for freedom.

World War II ends.
Evil Germany defeated.
A world safe for Democracy.
It made me remember FDR's election
and his New Deal as a child.
People bursting with hope and joy
along the parade route down Pennsylvania Avenue.
In the dense crowd, unable to see above
the thick wall of adult people,
I felt a sense of fear and the panic
of being knocked to the ground
and trampled underfoot amid all that joy.

Now, today I feel the weight and crush of this
fork-tongued Democracy experienced as prison,
the new slave plantation.
Night coming down.
John Brown entangled with soldiers' feet
kicked to the curb.
That's what I keep seeing!
A revolutionary flying as if he had wings,
metamorphosed as today's intellectual Abolitionist
on the move for exposure and liberation.

A poem written in response to Etheridge Knight's "Belly Song"

Harun F.

BELLY SONG

You have made something
Out of the sea that blew
And rolled you on its salt bitter lips.
It nearly swallowed you.
But I hear
You are tough and harder to swallow than most.

Harder to swallow than most.
Harder to swallow than Castor Oil.
Harder to swallow than the bitter truth.

Heard tell you wouldn't curtsy for the Queen.
Said a simple nod would do.

They say you jilted a Duke
You said he was too old,
Too fat, his breath stank, and he snored.

No amount of adoration,
Money,
Or station in life could make you suffer
That for the rest of your life.
You were free and would stay that way.

I spoke to some people who claim to know you.
They seemed disappointed that you are tough
As if the bashful way you drop your gaze,
Your easy smile, and gentle touch
Are only designed to deceive.

A poem written in response to Jared Carter's "The Purpose of Poetry"

James T.

INSPIRATION/REVELATION

Instinctively,
the unrecognized poet stirred in my soul,
and I grew apace
suddenly confident...
as if in a moment of awakening
to an exciting venture of
learning,
and creating
and expressing what I feel
yet untold from within my being
in verse
after reading and learning
that
The purpose of poetry is to tell us about life.

A poem written in response to Charles Simic's "Two Dogs"

Termaine J. H.

TWO OLD WINOS

Passing by this stoop, an Old Wino with a cheap bottle of beer
Told me he had a story to tell that he thought I ought to hear.
About an African boy who swore enmity between his people and a powerful nation
He nearly brought them to subjugation.
He was a Black King.
Was it of Pop? The King of New York?
Man, this drunk doesn't know a thing.
Between swigs of his brew
He remembered Hannibal Barca and his 3 brothers, known as the "Lion's Brood"
Descendants of the Queen of Carthage,
He was Commander of a rag-tag army known for its carnage.
The Romans were smug
As Hannibal marched over the Alps swift as a slug.
With elephants trekking paths not that wide,
Fighting through the elements and tribes,
Conquering Roman armies, the empire's pride.
He strolled to the city gates,
The citizens in wonder, their mouths agape
Hollering, "Hannibal's at the gates! Hannibal's at the gates!"
His promise to his father would have held true,
Had his resources from Africa made it through.
In agony, he retraced to his home town
Where the Romans regained their dignity
Burned Carthage to the ground.
I looked up. An eagle hovering above caught my eye.
Then Air Force One flew by;

It made me remember the stories my Grandmother told,
How Black Men, Women and Children were enslaved, bought and sold.
Raped. Lynched. Mutilated. Degraded. Castrated. Segregated.
Assassinated. Nearly annihilated.
Have we really made it?
Have the promises from over two thousand years ago come true?
Black President of a powerful nation who looks just like you.
Black Queen of Media.
Black Entrepreneurs.
Millionaires and Billionaires
But can't feed the poor.
I swear,
If Hannibal was here
He would shake his head in despair
From the disenfranchisement to which his people cling
Whatever happened to, "I have a Dream" and "Lift Every Voice and Sing"?
Martin Luther King's Dream could be Barack's reality.
But Malcom's Inspiration and Revolutionary qualities?
DIED, when the Men turned on their OWN with brutality…(sighs)
Tupac against Biggie. Karenga against Huey.
The futility behind it all.
The Old Wino on the stoop brought me back to reality when he stood tall,
Swaying and offered me a swig of his cheap beer,
I guzzled. Wiped my mouth, then said,
"I have a story to tell, would you like to hear"?

A poem in response to Etheridge Knight's "Belly Song"

D. Saadiq P.

BLUE SEA

What's up Son?
I see you, but you don't see me.
Damn, my bad. This ain't about me seeing you
or you seeing me.
I'm not talking about the sea
that separates a piece of land from another.

This about the sea of deep misery,
that has you locked up, boxed up
like the cargo in boats that float
over the sea to lands that seems like make
believe to me you see.

I can't be with you
to hold you and mold you like
a captain and his first mate.

But at any rate I can try to
guide you and steer you from
falling into the sea of the never-
ending abyss.

No fish, No coral, No islands
but plenty of salt, that comes
from the water that leaks
from the eyes of those who
secretly shed tears out of fear of
never escaping the Abyss.

The Abyss. I say it again
cuz it's not your friend,
this water, not blue or green,
that seems to come to life when you enter
like movie screens
with beautiful colors that shake and shimmer
as the Sun illuminates every glimmer.

Naw, son, this is the Black sea,
the deep dark place where
you don't wanna be.
Where everyone looks and feels like me
full of pain and despair in this
sea of stale air.
Take heed to my words or this
will be your destiny, because the
road you're heading down
has already got the best of me.

So I hope you see what I didn't see
and follow the Blue sea
and not the Black sea that has
swallowed me.

A poem written in response to William Stafford's "Traveling Through the Dark"

Michael W.

OLD TIMES

While traveling through the dark on a lonely bus, I find myself thinking back to when I was a child, when my mother used to hold me in her arms and tell me she loved me. My father would come home from work and tuck me into bed and tell me he loved me. Those were the happy times. Then came the abuse, the lying, and the not caring. I stopped being tucked in and told, "I love you." My father stopped coming home and my mother stayed out late. It was like a war zone with both of them in the house together. They would fight and argue all day; I would sit in my room and play my music loud to blur them out. There's nothing in the world that I wouldn't do to go back into time where I knew love and happiness was there.

A poem written in response to William Stafford's "Traveling Through the Dark"

Termaine J. H.

I COULD HEAR THE WILDERNESS LISTEN

At 3:49 am on December 14, 2012, I could hear the wilderness listen to thoughts conjured up by this gunman as he traveled in the dark from Willingborough, New Jersey to Newtown, Connecticut with evil intentions of doing the unimaginable at Sandy Hook Elementary School as his mother lay dead in her bed

At 6:15 am I could hear the wilderness listen to Caroline, age six, hum her favorite song between mouthfuls of cereal as her legs swung back and forth enthusiastically at the thought of all the fun she would have with her friends at school

At 7:28 am I could hear the wilderness listen to Justin Pinto's mother tell him he couldn't wear his favorite Victor Cruz New York Giants jersey to school today because he'd worn it the day before. Reluctantly, he took it off

At 7:30 am I could hear the wilderness listen to the other eighteen kindergartners as they sluggishly or happily rolled out of bed, brushed their teeth, ate their breakfast, hugged then told their parents "I love you" after being dropped off at school

At 9:05 am I could hear the wilderness listen to the labored breathing of the gunman as he methodically loaded the thirty-round magazine of his Bushmaster AR-15 assault rifle, the "click" and "clack" of metal and plastic as he checked then rechecked his Glock and Sig Saure 9mm pistols while he forged through the woods to Sandy Hook Elementary School

At 9:14 am I could hear the wilderness listen to the pupils of Victoria Soto laughing, carrying-on, singing their favorite songs as they marched through the halls of Sandy Hook Elementary School

At 9:26 am I could hear the wilderness listen to the explosion caused by the gunman's boot as he kicked in the front door to Sandy Hook Elementary School

At 9:28 am I could hear the wilderness listen to the frantic cries of teachers as their parental instincts kicked in and they began to usher and shield the frightened, fearful, confused kindergartners to safety while the menacing gunman stood chopping away at them

At 9:29 am I could hear the wilderness listen to heroic principal, Dawn Hochsprung, exit her office, imploring teachers to get their children to safety as she ran towards the gunman's line of fire, her body momentarily absorbing a barrage of bullets, saving dozens more

At 9:30 am I could hear the wilderness listen to the terror, screams, loud pleas for mercy as the gunman stood over Victoria Soto, who was huddled around her pupils as the gunman gunned her and her entire class of Kindergartners down

At 9:32 am I could hear the wilderness listen as the story broke across mass media that there was a shooting at an elementary school in Newtown, Connecticut

At 9:33 am I could hear the wilderness listen as the first responders entered Sandy Hook Elementary School silently as they saw lifeless kindergartners' bodies lying throughout the halls

At 9:35 am the wilderness became louder than usual to muffle the single shot of the gunman as he shot himself in the head

At 11:49 am I could hear the wilderness listen as President Barack

Obama paused at his press conference to wipe away the tears he couldn't hold back when describing the ages and method used to take these children's lives

I wonder, could the wilderness have done more than just listen?

Suggestions for Writing

1. Write something, an essay, poem, short story, short play, etc., based on some art object (a painting, photograph, music, a novel, a poem, etc.) that you have seen, heard, or read.

2. Describe a time when you were surprised by your own strength, mental or physical, or both.

About the Editors

Jayne Thompson

Jayne Thompson, a creative writing and English instructor at Widener University, began running a workshop for the Prison Literacy Project at S.C.I. Graterford in February of 2011. She is a Youth Aid Panelist for the Center for Resolutions, and through this group hears the cases of juvenile offenders in Chester, PA. In addition, she runs a writing center in Chester for high school students. She believes that reading and writing create avenues to freedom.

Emily DeFreitas

Emily DeFreitas is a member of Widener University's Presidential Service Corps, a group of high-achieving students who dedicate 300 hours per year to socially responsible leadership projects. She is a junior creative writing and English major who is currently at work on her first novel. She is originally from central New Jersey, and writes both poetry and fiction. This is her first time co-editing a book, and she has greatly enjoyed the experience.

About the Cover Artist

Leslie Herman

Leslie Herman is an award winning illustrator based out of Chicago, IL. You can view more of his work at www.leslieherman.com.

Anthology Contributors

Ronald J. C.

Born in 1944 in an orphanage, I was placed in numerous foster homes and juvenile institutions until I was eighteen. By court order, I entered the Army in 1962, and left in 1965. I was locked up in 1971. Since then, while serving a life sentence, I acquired my G.E.D and Associate Degree, and I became a writer and artist.

Charles K. D.

I was born on October 22, 1950. My parents taught us seven children that education was the key to success. As a child growing up in an all-white community, I experienced early racism. I also read and wrote a great deal at home and at school. My interest in writing has always been deep. Discovering myself while growing up in Philadelphia benefitted me tremendously. Freedom, peace and the necessity of family are as much a part of my existence as food.

Elliott E.

My name is Elliott E. I write because I have a voice that I believe should be heard. Writing also gives me structure and discipline. It forces me to work at being the best writer I can be. Plus, writing always stands the test of time. It is around many years after one has passed on. I am also the author of the book *Young and Incarcerated*.

Harun F.

I was born on August 18, 1944 in Mercy Douglas Hospital, in Philadelphia where I was raised. I am the fourth child of Gladys and Robert, the first born up north. I have an older sister, two older brothers and a baby sister. I went to West Philadelphia High School and enlisted in the Army from there. I married my childhood sweetheart, Linda, in 1967. We have three children, two girls and a boy, five grand children and one great grand. I am an Industrial Gas Plant Operator by trade and an entrepreneur by profession. I have been incarcerated since 1979. I lead a very fulfilling life and have a promising future.

Razzaqq "Raf" G.

Razzaqq "Raf" G. is a native of South Philadelphia. When a pencil hit a sheet of light yellow construction paper in the 2nd grade, Razzaqq felt at home writing, an activity that has been his home and freedom no matter where he has ended up. Incarcerated since age 19 and on the tail end of his prison term, Razzaqq has done years of work to change his life. He has become well known in the Philadelphia area Restorative Justice and Alternative to Violence communities and has recently begun to look into doing work to fight against human trafficking. He hopes that telling his story will aid other youths in choosing a better way early in life rather than when it's too late.

Termaine J. H.

Termaine J. H. grew up in Philadelphia. In 2005 he wrote his first stage play. In the fall of 2011, he met Jayne Thompson through her creative writing class at Graterford. His first assignment was to write a "semicolon poem" in one week. Up until this point he had never considered writing poetry. "Two Old Winos" is his first poem. Termaine is devoted to keeping youth out of trouble. So when Jayne informed him about a book she was compiling encouraging youth to "think twice" before doing something with grave consequences, he was more than willing to contribute in any way he possibly could.

Mwandishi M.

While incarcerated, Mwandishi M. realized he had a talent for creative writing. Besides pursuing his writing career, he continues his court fight. A published author, Mwandishi has two books, *The Prodigal Son* and *The Prodigal Son 2*.

Christopher R. M.

Hello! My name is Christopher R. M., and I'm a native of West Philadelphia. When I first arrived behind prison walls in January of 1983 (at age nineteen), I was functionally illiterate. In less than a year of imprisonment, I got my diploma and attended some college courses – despite being heavily drugged with psychotropics. I have I been blessed to regain a lucid mind, and I transcribe my thoughts on paper to heal myself. If my writings touch another's soul, then praise G-d. I pray that my writings touch you emotionally, soothe your mind, and impact your inner spirit.

D. Saadiq P.

D. "Saadiq" P. is an aspiring author and has read close to four-thousand books of various genres. In 1984, Saadiq's sixth grade English teacher, a paraplegic named Mr. Hoffman, introduced him to the world of Edger Allen Poe. His mother gave him his first novel, *Kaffir Boy* by Mark Mathabane about a young black boy growing up under apartheid in South Africa.

September of 1995 would have been the start of his freshman year at Penn State University, but an unfortunate event during that summer put Saadiq's dreams on hold. He leaves youths with this thought: "I had dreams of getting a degree from Pennsylvania State University, but somehow, I lost my way and now I am getting a degree from Pennsylvania State Penitentiary! I definitely would prefer the former over the latter, wouldn't you? Don't make the same mistakes I made. Don't be another me."

Winfield P.

For the past 37 years, I have been in the care and custody of the Department of Justice. I was born in 1956 and began this journey in 1977, all the while searching for a way to regain my freedom and life beyond the action and event that has cost me and separated me from family, friends, and positive life opportunities. I am reminded that every choice we have and decision we make has a consequence and cost attached to it. One that is too much to pay. . .

Paul J. P.

Paul J. P. is serving a life sentence at Graterford Prison. Born in Philadelphia on April 26, 1956, he has been incarcerated since the age of nineteen. Throughout most of his incarceration, Paul has taken advantage of various self-improvement opportunities, earning associate's and bachelor's degrees and completing a host of other educational programs. In 2008, he received the Pennsylvania Prison Society's Prisoner of the Year Award, acknowledging his leadership, many contributions, and efforts to improve the lives of others within and beyond the prison community.

Eduardo R.

"I want action!" So says Eduardo R. –ex-vandal, poet, artist, and humanist. Born in Philly, but raised in prison, Eddie has managed the superhuman feat of maintaining his dignity despite tremendous opposition. His approach to literature is rooted in the belief that the word, whether written or spoken, can be used as an arrow that protects the archer and defends against the wolf – for the world is full of wolves.

Writing as a form of protest against forces who would otherwise suppress the voices of liberation, Eddie speaks through his characters, using a wide range of emotions to describe a world that is more real than real.

Frank R.

Frank R., a ninth-grade dropout, learned to write fiction during his incarceration. Against all odds, he finally published his first short story, "Mister Milhouser" in Joan Silva's fine journal, *The Signal*. He has sold dozens of other stories across the country. Still without an agent, he's unable to get his collection, Nora's Trials and Tribulations & Other Stories into a publishing house. Mr. R. has been writing mostly screenplays for the last five years, and he hopes to get into a production company. He is seeking help from the reading public to get his work into the right people's hands.

Kempis S.

Kempis was born in Port of Spain, Trinidad and Tobago, on February 5, 1972. After exemplary school performance and no problems with the law, Kempis ran away from his home in Brooklyn to Philadelphia, a week before completing 9th grade. He was incarcerated at age 15. During his 26 years (and counting) of incarceration, Kempis has continued his education, reading and writing avidly. He has earned his certification as a personal trainer and is a student in the Villanova-Graterford college program. A writer of poetry, short stories, memoirs, and essays—and a devoted student in Professor Jayne's Widener writing class— Kempis (also affectionately known as Ghani) leapt at the opportunity to help steer young people from the path that leads to prison. "Writing is releasing," and "You gotta write for what's right," are two mantras he lives by.

James T.

James T. was born in Washington, DC, on December 20, 1941. In 1971, when he was 29 years old, he received a life sentence. James is a trained dental technician, and also has an Associate Degree in Business from The Pennsylvania Business Institute. He is a writer of short stories, poems and essays, and is the founder of People Advancing Reintegration (PAR), an inmate self-help program that helps fellow prisoners prepare for their freedom. He is currently pursuing his freedom through the courts in hopes of winning his freedom and carrying on the work of this organization as a free man.

Michael W.

I was born and raised in South Philly. I'm 28, and I have been in prison for 96,096 hours. That's 11 years—since I was 16. Growing up was hard. My pops wasn't around and my mom was working too hard. I have a 10-20 year sentence. Coming to prison helped me to appreciate my freedom and life more. I got educated and met some people who were willing to give me another chance. All this time I spent in prison, someone has told me when to eat, sleep, and go to the bathroom. Coming to prison saved me from a lot of things, but it is the worst thing that has ever happened to me.

Aaron C. W.

Aaron C. W., an unpublished writer, has been imprisoned for well over two decades. Since 2002, he has suffered from an incurable form of chronic lymphoblastic leukemia (CLL/cancer). He survived two rounds of chemotherapy, in 2009 and 2013. He continues to educate and help others through his good deeds, love, and writing, such as this well-thought-out warning that he offers you in this book. If his message prevents one person from falling into the conspiracy trap, he knows he has contributed something good to society and youths.

AFTERWORD

Thomas E. Kennedy, M.F.A, Ph.D.

HUMANITARIANS AT THE GRATE:
The Writing Group at Graterford Maximum Security Prison

"There are such helpers in the world, who rush to save
anyone who cries out."
—Rumi (translated by Coleman Barks)

The State Correctional Institution at Graterford is located in Skippack Township, Montgomery County, Pennsylvania, near Graterford, about thirty-one miles west of Philadelphia. The facility, built in 1929, is the state's largest maximum security prison with upward of 5,000 prisoners in 3,200 individual cells on 1,730 acres of farmland. The prison includes a death row section, although executions have never been carried out in this facility. Prisoners are usually two to a cell.

Since the beginning of 2011, Jayne Thompson—a senior lecturer at Widener University in Chester, whose creative writing department supports her activities in the prison—has been mentoring a group of about twenty mostly life-sentence prisoners here, between the ages of 25 and 80, once a week for an hour and a half in addition to the hour and a half she drives each way from her home. Some of the men were sentenced to life via a mandatory life-sentence statute for having been present, or in the getaway vehicle, when a robbery went from bad to worse and someone was killed. Although Jayne could find out what the men are in for—it is a matter of public record—she doesn't want to know. Nonetheless, she knows that among the crimes for which the men have been convicted is murder. She does know that perhaps four of them have a sentence less than life and that a twenty-five year old who has been in since he was sixteen will get out next year. When I think of the changes that took place in the past decade—many of which I, a free man, can hardly keep up with—I can't imagine how it will be for him, locked away from ten years of quantum advancement in quotidian technology.

We pull into the parking area outside the administration building, and I empty my pockets to leave wallet, keys, money, cell phone in the car, slide off my belt—none of which are allowed into the prison. Alongside the administration building, a modern structure of brick and glass, a solid thirty-foot rebar-reinforced concrete wall looms up. At the end, a rifleman watches from a glass-windowed turret. The wall surrounds the 62-acre prison compound, surmounted by nine such manned towers. Eddie R. (see page 64 of this book), a member of the prison writing group, will later confide, "That wall is symbolic to us. What does it make you think of?" In fact, it makes me think of the hopelessness of ever getting through or over or around it.

We walk toward the building, through which we will have to pass to enter the prison compound. The reason for my presence is that Jayne has invited the men in the writers' group to read my novel *In the Company of Angels*, about a Chilean torture survivor being treated in the torture rehabilitation center in Copenhagen and getting involved with a woman who has herself survived domestic abuse. The question of the novel, to which I attempted to discover the answer by writing the book, is whether two people who have survived such darkness are capable of experiencing love again. Jayne and I have been preparing for my visit for many months. There was considerable preliminary paperwork—including a disclaimer of liability which I had to sign—as well as the mechanics of getting the books to the prisoners. Discovering that Amazon.com had a special limited-time offer of two dollars a copy, postage included, I arranged to have twenty sent to Jayne. I thought it might be pleasing to the "guys" (as Jayne refers to them) to have hardbacks, but that complicated matters. The lieutenant of the guard was reluctant to allow so many hard covers into the facility. Apparently a hard cover can be fashioned into a weapon. Even scotch tape is prohibited. But eventually, thanks to Jayne's cheerful, patient persistence, the administration granted permission, and the men were allowed to receive the books.

This is the first in the visiting writer and scholar series that Jayne has started. Next will be the chairman of Widener's creative writing department, Dr. Michael Cocchiarale, and a young Joyce scholar, Dr. Janine Utell. I will probably have one and a half hours with the guys.

"Our time slot is six to eight," Jayne says, "but I can never be sure when the guard escort will arrive. It may be right away, but even if the guard walks me down on time, the men might be held up. In fact, they may come in very late, singly, here and there. They get held back sometimes for one thing or another." When she speaks vaguely about it, I understand that she is glossing over the mechanics of prison bureaucracy, trying not to jeopardize the existence of the writers group. I ask no questions.

During the time available, I hope to do a brief talk about how I started writing, a twenty-five minute reading, a Q&A, and also talk to them about the book they are writing collectively and Jayne Thompson and Emily DeFreitas are editing this book, *Letters to My Younger Self*. Members of the group will write a letter to their younger selves, when they were between eleven and seventeen years old about a choice they made that had negative consequences on their lives. They will also write about the experience of being in prison, what led them there. Serving House Books—a small, non-profit house co-published by Walter Cummins and myself (www.ServingHouseBooks.com) will issue it as soon as it is ready. The aim is to get it out among potential or early juvenile offenders, to help them get straight before they do something irrevocable; it will be a significant contribution by the guys to society. Jayne has access to many "juvies" through her volunteer service for the Center for Resolutions, once a month, hearing the cases of juvenile offenders and deciding their "penalties"—often a writing assignment.

Her position in the Center for Resolutions (http://www. center4resolutions.org/), a semi-public initiative supplementary to the court system dealing with conciliation and "restorative justice," is in a Youth Aid Panel Program, providing juvenile offenders the opportunity to go before a panel of trained community members who work with them—where violator and victim agree—to create a resolution which holds them accountable for their violation, encourages them to make amends, includes an educational component and often recommends community service. Juveniles who successfully complete the Youth Aid Panel Program have all charges removed from their record and are given a second chance. *Letters to My Younger Self* would be offered as an educational component of the Panel.

Jayne had been looking into getting a young man she taught at Chester High School to help her with the art work and editing, at which he is exceptionally proficient, but he has disappeared into the system, and she is having difficulty finding him. She has heard that he was arrested in possession of a handgun and put into a juvie lock-up. His nickname is "Blaze," and the guys have told her that nickname is sometimes given to a person who has killed someone. So Paul J. P., the Internal Director of the Prison Literacy Project (mentoring fellow inmates who are unable to read), has enlisted an inmate at Graterford to assist with the artwork for the book.

At the foot of the steps to the administration building is a blackboard-sized sign setting out the prohibitions and regulations on the premises—essentially, that visitors will be treated with the respect that they are expected to accord to the prison personnel, that abusive language or behavior will not be tolerated, that illicit substances are not permitted. We linger in front of the sign; because I cannot photograph it and feel conspicuous copying it in short hand, I am trying to memorize it. A guard climbs down the wheelchair ramp toward us, leaning backward into the slant. "What are you doing?" he asks.

"Just reading the rules," Jayne says neutrally, "I'm a volunteer—teaching in the reading group which meets tonight. We're from Widener University, and we teach a writing group here..." Out the side of her mouth, she whispers to me, "Sometimes too much information is good," and we ascend the eight steps, his eyes on us, to the building's double-gated airlock-type main entrance. Thursday is also visiting day so there is a line of family members standing before the registration desk. To the left is a cluster of benches on which a few women sit, a few children, a few children's books scattered along the seats—a Donald Duck jumbo book. I think of the Beagle Boys.

Jayne swipes her fingerprint card through a device mounted on the wall, and we move to stand in front of yet another thick sliding door, with chipped beige paint and a window of dense glass, waiting for the door to slide open. After a few moments, it does, and Jayne introduces me to the guard there. I offer my hand, and he takes it, giving me the eye, and I give him my photo ID. The guard, a short beefy African-American man of about fifty, opens a thick book and asks Jayne, "He here just this one time?"

"Yes," she says agreeably, flashing her Jayne smile. "We did all the paperwork months ago."

He flips through the book, locates a pouch with a deep swatch of pages, begins slowly, meticulously to leaf through them. Jayne and I glance tensely at one another. She has told me that paperwork sometimes gets lost in the shuffle. I am thinking how close I am to meeting the guys yet there are still many more thick doors between us and them. I begin to fear that I will not be let in, can see in Jayne's eyes we share that fear. I plan to ask her to go ahead in if I'm kept out, to at least tell the men I was here, that I tried to keep my promise, to ask her to give them my best wishes, tell them I am waiting outside.

Then the guard says, "Here it is."

He stamps the back of our hands with an ink that is only visible under the ultraviolet light of a scanner lamp; when we come out again we will place our hands under that lamp once more and if the light doesn't cause the stamp to fluoresce, we will potentially be considered escapees.

Next is the metal detector, above which is a sign instructing people not to hop, jump or run through. I am told to remove my leather coat and sweater and place my folder and book on the table. My pockets are already empty, and my pants, beltless, repeatedly have to be hitched up. I also place my thermal vest on the table, and the guard says, "You don't have to take the lining out your jacket." I tell him it's not attached. Alertly, he asks, "Not attached? Then you got to leave it here. Pick it up on you way out." But after I pass through the metal detector without ringing a bell, I am allowed to pull my sweater on again. I wonder what difference the vest would have made. The guard minutely examines the padding of my leather coat, flips through the pages of my book, opens my folder, leafs through it, pushes his fingers into the pouches.

Then he ties a white bracelet around my wrist, says, "You don't get out without that bracelet is still on you," provides a visitor's badge that clips to the collar of my sweater. We wait in front of another thick sliding door for a guard to escort us in. The door slides open and a short, slight guard appears; his face is strikingly strange, seemingly utterly devoid of humor. He motions us to wait. Up ahead of us, perhaps fifteen feet, is a chain-link wall with an open gate.

"Very unusual," Jayne says softly. "Both the door and the gate are open."

My ears, my head, are filled with the sounds of buzzers, echoing noises, sliding doors that slam with a bang. You could never break down a door like that; you could hardly even knock on it without bruising your knuckles. Looking through the open door and gate, I see prisoners and guards milling around inside the mouth of a long, wide hallway dotted with metal detectors in front of other doors to left and right. Some of the prisoners are filing into the visitors' room. The guards wear different colored tunics and peaked caps—white or blue-grey. The prisoners wear brown jackets with large letters on back: D.O.C. "For some of us," one of the inmates will later mention, "that brown color has racial implications."

An extremely tall black guard, an officer I think, perhaps a lieutenant, greets Jayne with a warm smile. She tells me that he is a poet himself. "Mostly spoken word. Poetry slam kind of thing."

The guard with the strange face signals us to follow him. I wonder if he is really devoid of humor or whether his deadpan is a response to his job, his surroundings, his life, his childhood. I mention his face later, and one of the inmates says, "Do you think ugliness is drawn to ugly environments—or maybe ugly environments strip away handsomeness."

Behind the guard, very slowly we walk the long, broad hallway, which I estimate is two hundred yards long and perhaps twenty or thirty yards wide with doors here and there along it—doors to the visitors' room, to cell blocks, to the chapel. There are also windows, and Jayne points out to the yard where the men exercise and lift weights.

"That's where Ghani—one of the members of the writing group—showed me that there's a nesting goose with a gosling in the nest. The guys take care of it. He was so happy to show me that." Outside another window she points out a baseball diamond where the men play ball in good weather.

I am surprised by the seeming disorganized comings and goings of the prisoners and surprised to be so close to them, with no walls or bars between us. Jayne told me she once forgot and walked that hallway before the guard escort had arrived, and she was scolded by both the guards and the guys; she risked losing the privilege of teaching here for a carelessness of that nature.

Trying not to be too direct, I observe the men out of the corners of my eyes. I see one short muscular man bump shoulders, hard, with a passing, younger, fellow inmate and remember when I was a kid growing up in Queens how I hated being required to try to fake that toughness, remember the last fistfight I had, at fourteen, how brutal it had been, how Vinnie Teofilo and I had rolled over desks in the classroom on a break, punching each other's face repeatedly. I recall seizing his hair and drawing back his head to get in a better punch, how afterwards I realized that no one wins a fight like that, that John Wayne notwithstanding, nothing is gained from it, only a lessening of your humanity, and I risked the designation of "faggot" and "punk" by resolving to try to be a pacifist. I wonder what that resolution would do for me here, whether I would have the courage to carry it through.

A young, tall African-American man, muscular, struts past, and it occurs to me that if somehow I was imprisoned here, that if it had gone the wrong way I might have ended in a place like this, and I might not last, probably wouldn't. Later I happen to mention this, and a member of the inmates writing group says, "Consider that innocent men and women have been subjected to this intimidating environment."

Finally the guard stops at a door over which is a sign—Education. He unlocks it. There is a hall, two guards seated at a desk about twenty feet away. The guards are both African American—a thick-shouldered man in his late forties perhaps with a smiling face, wearing a white tunic, and a young woman who couldn't be more than early twenties, wearing a blue-grey uniform. The uniform jacket has half sleeves, revealing her bare forearms on which dark-blue linear designs are tattooed into the dark skin, from her elbows down—maybe above, too. She has long black wavy curls and a sweet, shy smile. "I never met a famous author before," she says.

"I'm not famous."

"You famous to me," she says. Her smile is so sweet and shy that I wish I could sit and chat with her for half an hour. There are so many things I would like to ask about her life, but there is no time for that.

A number of men, mostly African-American, are placing passes on the desk and entering the door of the room we'll meet in. Jayne has told me that being in prison is like being in high school—you have to get a pass for everything.

A little way from the desk, Jayne and I enter a large room full of men, most of whom are carrying my novel. Each in turn approaches to greet me, shake my hand, introduce himself. Too many names to remember with a fit to each face, but the names themselves read a little bit like African-American poetry—D. Saadiq P. (pages 29, 51 and 155 of this book), Eddie R. (page 64), Termaine H. (pages 32, 84 and 153), Ghani (Kempis S.) (page 80), Michael W. (pages 25 and 157), Winfield P. (pages 107, 108, 112 and 132), Aaron C. W. (page 70), Jesse F., Elliott E. (page 110), Charles D. (page 27), Frank R. (pages 105 and 106), Ronald J. C.—who is called "RC" (page 126), Harun F. (pages 78 and 151), Mwandishi M. (page 55), Christopher M. (pages 19, 62 and 112), James (Muhammed) T. (pages 22, 133, 149 and 152), Paul J. P. (pages 9, 31, 36, 43 97 and 121) ... Harun F.—who Jayne calls "Mr. H. F."—has a beard and hair of white and gray—Aaron is much younger, only a couple of strands of gray in his wild, bushy beard. Paul J. P., as well as being a mentor to fellow inmates who cannot read, is also a member of the Lifers Public Safety Initiative. RC—the only white man among them—refers to this writing and reading group as "Humanitarians at the Grate"—Grate, of course, is short for Graterford, and suggests a screen separating the men from the rest of humanity.

Chairs are arranged in a large oval formation, and one of the guys—Eddie R., a Latino poet—tells me that they have saved a chair for me at the head of the oval and indicates another one with a desk on which I can place my papers and book. (In a draft of this article, I will describe the group as all African Americans with only two white guys. In fact, Eddie is one of the guys I will describe as white—he is Latino; I will learn later that this will earn him the jocular nickname of "the other white guy.")

Jayne and I sit beside one another, and Paul J. P. sits to her left. She has told me that he always sits beside her; that is his seat as the man who has hand-picked all the members of this group. She has also told me that there will be no guard in the room. "Which is really good," she added. I agree. How could you discuss writing or freely read out what you've written under the eyes of a guard? I often quote the writer whose name I cannot remember who said, "One of the most important jobs for a writer is to catch the policeman in your mind asleep."

The tension I was not even aware of feeling is sliding from me at their warmth, at the clear welcome in their eyes, in their postures. I see that Eddie is seated beside me, the Latino fellow the fellow who told me about the desk; not tall but with a deep chest, hard shoulders, he looks friendly and tough, full of a restless energy, reminds me of a guy I grew up with in Queens. He sits off to my right on the other side of a black man named Saadiq, whose desk is to my right, about a foot behind me. I understand wanting to have your back to the wall.

Saadiq is young and tall, a beard squaring his jaw, bare from lower lip to chin. His eyes are dark, intense, and look directly into mine. The white man, named RC, is seated at the far left end of the oval, tall and lean. All the others in the room save Jayne and me are African-American. It reminds me of my days in the army, in basic training, where nearly half the men were black, one of the opportunities for a black person in those days.

The percentage of African-Americans in U.S. prisons is vastly disproportionate to their percentage in the general population. The total U.S. prison population, according to Wikipedia, quoting U.S. Bureau of Justice statistics, is the highest documented rate in the world with 743 adults incarcerated per 100,000 population—in all at the end of 2010, 2,266,800 adults were in prison in the U.S., and nearly 40% of them were African-American with over 20% Hispanic. By contrast, only about 13% of the U.S. population is African-American and only about 13% Latino.

When we are all seated, I have a moment of uncertainty—what happens now—but remember something that Jayne told me Paul J. P. said to her once—"You are in charge." So I start, by conveying greetings from Inge Genefke and Bent Sørensen, who called me the day before I left, to be certain I remembered to send their greetings to the prisoners. I tell the men that Inge and Bent have spent decades, most of their professional lives, fighting against torture and trying to help rehabilitate torture survivors, raising money for the anti-torture movement. Through Jayne, I give Paul J. P. three copies of *The Meeting with Evil: Inge Genefke's Fight against Torture*, a selection of reworked chapters from her biography by Thomas Larsen which I have introduced and translated from the Danish (Serving House Books, 2010). It also includes an interview with Bent Sørensen, who for many years, as a U.N. Rapporteur, visited prisons in countries which were signatories to the UN Convention against Torture, to try to intervene if he detected signs of torture being used. I promise Paul to send additional copies of the book to Graterford through Jayne.

As agreed with Jayne, I address the group about how I began to love reading when I was fifteen years old and my father gave me a book by Dostoyevsky. I was instantly hooked on it and from that day forth was an avid reader. Actually the book was *Crime and Punishment*, but I refrain from mentioning the title for fear the guys might think there is a subtext to the message. I ask whether anyone in the group has read anything by Dostoyevsky, and several murmur titles—*The Brothers Karamazov, Crime and Punishment, The Idiot...*

Ghani, light-skinned and slender, sitting off about halfway down the oval on the right with his magnificent dreadlocks, even two or three dreads in his long beard, says distinctly, "The House of the Dead."

"That is an amazing book," I agree, remembering when I was sixteen and read it, completely absorbed by it. I wish that I could find words to express how much I appreciated that book—about Dostoyevsky's four years in a penal colony—to a man who is living that life for far more than four years. My imagination fails me. I realize that the policeman in my own mind is patrolling my thoughts before I speak them—but this policeman is well-intentioned, he is trying to do the right thing, what he whispers to me is that these men do not have their freedom, that that is their burden and that I must not do anything to contribute to that burden. Rather I should attempt to try and lighten that burden, to try to help them see how writing and literature can make them, as Alain de Botton puts it in *The Consolations of Philosophy*, healthier and happier.

For me, I tell them, discovering reading was like discovering an invisible door in the little bedroom I slept in as a kid—a door that I never knew was there before and through which I could enter into the minds of others who had made them accessible by writing a book, and through those books, I could enter into my own mind as well. I tell about how at the age of seventeen, a short story by Katherine Mansfield, "Miss Brill," so deeply moved me that I decided the only thing I wanted to do in life was to write—to discover what was in my own mind and heart and to share it with others. That is my spiritual discipline. But it took me so long to get anything published—twenty years—that I tried to quit writing, even sold my books to a second hand bookshop to get them out of my sight, but started missing them and buying them back.

The guys laugh with understanding.

"Must have cost you a fortune to get 'em back," Winfield—tall, with elegant dreadlocks, says with a friendly smile.

It took me twenty years to learn to write, I tell them, but then I finally published a story and became familiar with the place that my stories came from and they came more quickly and many more stories and books followed. Something I read in the diary of Dostoyevsky, written when he was eighteen years old and which I read when I was eighteen, nearly a hundred years later, seems it might be of interest to them: "Man is a mystery. This mystery must be solved, and even if you pass your whole life solving it, do not say that you have wasted your time. I occupy myself with this mystery because I want to be a man."

As agreed with Jayne, I read three scenes from my novel that they have read—the first chapter, which contains a flashback of Bernardo being tortured; the chapter midway through where Bernardo first meets Michela Ibsen and dances a tango with her; and the scene where Nardo tells the story about how when he was in prison, being tortured, and had not even seen the sky or the sun or had a breath of summer air for two years, and he wanted to give up, he was visited by two angels who took him out of the prison for a moment and let him feel the sun on his flesh, healing him, and promised that one day he would be released.

When I begin to read a section, I say what page in the book it starts on so that those who want can follow the text. It seems that they all do, but I cite the wrong page number on the last scene—166 instead of 163—and the younger, wild-bearded Aaron interrupts me, calling out urgently, "What page?!" as though I broke my half of the agreement.

"Start over!" says Ghani earnestly.

When I am finished reading, we have about forty minutes left, and I open the floor to discussion. Right off there is a dicey moment. Mike, a tall younger man, beard following the lines of a square jaw, stares directly, perhaps sharply into my eyes, and asks whether I chose the scenes I read for "a particular reason," the phrase dripping significance.

Whoa!

I thought they would enjoy that scene about the angels, but maybe I made a mistake choosing it; Mike seems to think so. Maybe some of them found it condescending or presumptuous—too "near-going," as the Danes say—impertinent.

"No, no reason," I deadpan. "I thought those scenes were good reading pieces, the images and the rhythm of the language. That's the only reason."

His face relaxes. He nods appeasingly, and the discussion takes off.

The younger Aaron comments that the the writing style includes very detailed description and symbolic use of names, words, places, events, and conversations which lodge them into his attention to help recall at a later recurrence. That is exactly what I tried to do and am impressed by the comment.

Ghani says a few words about my use of metaphors and similes, pointing out how in the tango scene I describe Nardo's and Michela's movements "like courting birds." He notes how just three words create a whole picture and discusses how it is necessary to use your eyes as a writer to observe and arrive at particular images.

Eddie asks how important I think a formal education is for an author. "Does a writer have to know all about realism and surrealism and magical realism and modernism and postmodernism, for example?"

I tell him it sounds like he already does, but emphasize that anything a writer knows will help him with his craft and his narrative and his characters and dialogue, that even if you only know a little bit about something, it can help. After all, a fiction writer only has to create the illusion of knowing in order to frame his narrative—that the knowledge that you impart through a book of fiction is less important than the wisdom you can find in it and that the wisdom is imparted through the interaction of your characters and of the narrative, via your use of language, how much of human experience it illuminates—your knowledge of the heart rather than of facts.

Mwandishi, off to my left, beefy and dark with an easy smile, asks if he might read aloud a scene he has highlighted from page 82:

> In the silence quiet piano notes and bass runs spoke and answered one another, with Miles Davis's trumpet saying, asking, Soooo what? Sooo what? So simple and simply until the horns of Cannonball Adderly and John Coltrane and Davis began to weave from that simplicity a more intricate pattern that lowered Voss's eyelids with the pleasure of the evening.

"You read that beautifully," I say, thinking how I could never have imagined when I wrote those lines eight years ago that I would one day be sitting here having them read aloud to me by a man who seemed to love them as much as I did, but spending his life in prison.

Mwandishi smiles, clearly pleased that I liked the way he read it. "I know that music," he says, then asks, "You like jazz? What kind?"

"Mostly bebop."

His smile deepens. "My man!" Later he will send me a four-page list of nearly 500 "must-hear" jazz titles that he urges me to listen to.

Then Paul J. P.—large and dark, with short hair and eyeglasses and a gentle air about him—wants to talk about Michela and how I felt about writing from a woman's point of view. Did any women complain that I got it wrong? Noticing a long scar on his neck—looks like someone might have tried to slit his throat, which makes my book seem far less interesting than this man, I tell him that was the first whole novel I ever wrote that didn't have any Americans in it and where a large part of the central intelligence in the book was a woman's. "But I trusted Michela. I fell in love with Michela."

Eyes smiling behind the lenses of his glasses, Paul says with quiet conviction, "We all fell in love with Michela."

"Me, too," Jayne adds and laughs her infectious laughter.

"No women complained about Michela," I say, "but a few complained about Voss, the drunken womanizer." Paul smiles and says just, "Voss," seeming to convey his view of Voss's clownishness as the behavior of a child, but Eddie adds, "I understand Voss. I see him as an honest, insecure character."

A tall, muscular man named Termaine, light-skinned and short-haired, asks about the quote that Nardo uses in the book: I do not create, I destroy. I chop ice. He asks it with a large, wide smile, as if it tickles him. At that moment, I cannot recall the name of the German writer who said that but promise to try to find out and tell it to Jayne to tell him. Termaine nods, satisfied. "I think it was the guy who wrote *The Three Penny Opera*, but I can't remember his name."

A man on the far side of the circle, Frank R., who is seventy-nine-years old and looks rather like Bill Cosby, says, "I think that was Kurt Weill."

"I think he wrote the music to *The Three Penny Opera*," I say. Afterward I realize the name I was groping for was Bertolt Brecht, but cannot remember whether he actually said that or not. Perhaps it was Kafka.—in fact, browsing through my books I just found a similar statement by Kafka: "A book ought to be an icepick to break up the frozen sea within us." But not quite. Maybe I made that up myself!

Frank R. will later send me an envelope of his writing, one page of which contains a beautiful 200-word prose poem about his yearning to touch a tree. (Please see page 106 of this book.)

"Do you ever have a feeling that your scene is too long, that it's taking too long to write it?" asks Terrell, short-haired, spectacles spanning his thin, dark-skinned face. I say if it feels too long it might be too long. But if you take the trouble to write it, you might be happy with it finally—or you can always take it out, or shorten it.

In their questions to me, about my craft, I feel we are having a conversation, that their questions reveal as much about them as my answers do about me. Maybe more, in fact. Because if a man in prison for a long time still cares about the art of literature and the craft of its creation, or has come to care about it, then that is a whole man, I think, a healthy man, a man with dignity, a man who will stay on his feet. His caring about these details will keep him alive, will help him not to despair—just as they help me not to despair.

Mwandishi asks hesitantly, when I say in the book that the Chilean junta had learned the art of torture from their neighbors to the north, "Did you mean...?"

I nod. "The CIA." And I want to ask what political beliefs he has, what all of them have, wondering what a man might think about a system that locks him up for the rest of his life—with ostensibly no hope of ever getting out alive—that locks so many black men up. Suddenly it all seems hopeless to me again. As hopeless as it did in 1961 when an older woman I had known and liked at work one day, when Fats Domino came on the radio, said, "Some nigger's driving a Cadillac off what he earns on that song," and I thought about how my parents never allowed us to say the N-word, and I thought there was no hope for my country, even a century after the Civil War, when ostensibly nice white people can say such a hateful thing based on the color of a man's skin. And Hoover bugged Martin Luther King, Jr., and then they killed him, shot him down, a brave visionary pacifist with a dream who would not back down... There seemed no hope. Then, when Obama was elected, I thought all that was over, but it is not over. Men are locked away for life because they inherit the effects of all this.

Maybe the best way to get out is to go deeper into yourself, I think.

Maybe through that undiscovered door inside your spirit. Maybe these men and I are all searching for the same thing. Maybe we are all prisoners inside our skulls.

As though he hears my thoughts, the white man, in the far corner of the oval, RC, asks how many languages I speak. I tell him two, English and Danish. "I used to almost speak French when I lived in France as a young man, good enough that I learned to flirt with the bakery girl I bought my morning bread from." I hear from their laughter that they like that.

Ghani asks whether I feel like a citizen of the world, now that I can write a book with so many different people in it, from so many different countries and not even one American. And it's true in a sense, I no longer feel completely American, but I'm not completely European either. I wish that I could have thought at that moment of what Alain de Botton quoted from Montaigne about Socrates in his book *The Consolations of Philosophy*—that when Socrates was asked where he was from he did not say "From Athens," but "From the world."

With a chuckle, Ghani mutters, "But you can flirt with that French bakery girl okay!" Which creates a ripple of laughter, and I remember at that moment palpably when I was in the army and lived with black men for the first time in my life, what good-natured, good companions most of them were. And I remember something Jayne told me about Terrell, one of the darkest guys in the group, beautifully black; how he had asked her, "You know what I didn't like about myself when I was young?" And pointed at his own hand, and she understood him to mean the color of his own skin.

What a turned-over world has affected these men! Increasingly it seems to me that I perceive black as the most beautiful color of skin, and ask myself how the bigotry against it could ever have developed other than from guilt, from crazy guilt about four hundred years of subjugating another race, of having to demonize the members of the race in order to justify the superiority that was presumed but was based on nothing but pure economic and social advantage. And in demonizing the members of the race, compelling some of them, a disproportionate percentage of them, to desperation and desperate acts.

Suddenly I notice that it is almost eight p.m., and we haven't even done the signing yet. Our time together has vanished—we could easily have used another hour or two. Mercifully the guard gives us an extra ten or fifteen minutes—an extraordinary occurrence I understand from Jayne, who has warned me not to request more time if the guards say that the time is up.

The men line up with their books. It takes a while because many of their names are foreign to my ear and have to be spelled for me. Misspelling a name when you are trying to personalize a book with a dedication is the quickest way to depersonalize it. Also I want to try to find something appropriate to write to each of them, this meeting has been so special to me, but it is difficult in so short a time. I ask if they want me to write "Graterford" on the dedication page, too—they do.

Ghani asks me to dedicate it to "the name my mother gave me—Kempis" because he wants to show the book to her.

When I've signed the last book we still have a couple of minutes left, and I stand chatting with a few of the men. My novel tucked under his arm, Eddie thanks me for my visit. "You know," he says. "Victor Hugo is said to be the perfect stylist. I think you surpass him." And with that, I begin to realize how much these men appreciate any gesture from the world outside. I remember how Jayne had told me that she brought them little notebooks in which to record their thoughts—she had not been allowed to bring in the pocket-sized spiral pads she bought at first, but found others that were not considered contraband, not considered potential weapons, and the men had been profoundly moved by the gift.

Eddie asks if I were writing a memoir and said that a man was running and fell in horseshit when in reality it was mud he fell in, whether I would consider that untrue. Jayne told me about a discussion at an earlier meeting of the group when Saadiq had written that someone fell in horseshit and later admitted that in fact it was mud, but thought it was more entertaining as horseshit. Saadiq stands off to the side chuckling.

Trying to be light, I say to Eddie, "I'd go for the horseshit," failing to realize how important the question was to him. I don't have enough time to explain to him my feeling that all writing contains a degree of untruth—because we have to select, arrange, leave things out, and simply because we cannot catch all of reality in language, have to settle for a small piece of it, but that the important thing, it seems to me, is not whether a man falls in horseshit or mud, but whether we are true to the essential facts, whether we are true to our heart and spirit and understanding. But that if it is important to Eddie whether someone fell in horseshit or mud, why then that is his own essential truth and I would salute him for being loyal to it. But I cannot think quickly enough to go into all of that, there is not enough time. Eddie says, "I only meant to get clarity on whether it is okay, when writing a memoir, to invent a detail for effect."

The men are returning to their cells. RC comes from his far corner of the room and tells me that he has an idea for a story. He will write a story from the point of view of the watch strapped to my wrist. "And then, as your watch, I'll be traveling with you to all the cities of the world you travel to, and I'll see all the places."

The lump in my throat will not give passage to the words of encouragement I want to say to him.

Ghani comes over just before he has to leave to ask if Serving House Books is still going to publish their book, and I realize suddenly that we never got to talk about that. "Absolutely," I say. "As soon as the book is ready, it will go to press."

Then the pretty young African-American guard is waiting to walk us out along the broad corridor, talking about a bookstore in Boyertown where I could do a reading, and I am disoriented to see Mr. H. F., as Jayne calls him, walking toward me with a smile. He shakes my hand again, his black white-bearded face, white-haired pate, tilted back a little—somehow I understand why Jayne only calls him "Mr. H. F." He deserves the title.

And then Jayne and I are shoving the backs of our hands under the ultraviolet lamp, to show that the validating stamps fluoresce, and we return our white bracelets and visitors badges and pass through three more doors—seven doors in all, from the classroom to the open night, and the guys will have to go through two or three more doors, deeper into the Grate.

Outside, Jayne says, "Thank you so much for doing this."

I tell her that the thanks are mine. "If it weren't for you, I could never have experienced this. You are doing beautiful work for those men, and I could see how much they appreciate it."

An image flashes in my mind of a poem by Rumi:

> A dragon was pulling a bear into its terrible mouth.
> A courageous man went and rescued the bear.
> There are such helpers in the world, who rush to save
> anyone who cries out. Like Mercy itself,
> they run toward the screaming,
> and they can't be bought off.
> If you were to ask one of those, "Why did you come
> so quickly?" he or she would say, "Because I heard…"

Thomas E. Kennedy's 30+ books include most recently his *Getting Lucky: New & Selected Stories, 1982-2012* and the four, highly praised books of the *Copenhagen Quartet,* four independent novels celebrating the seasons and souls of the Danish capital, all from Bloomsbury Publishing: *In the Company of Angels* (2010), *Falling Sideways* (2011), *Kerrigan in Copenhagen* (2013), and *Beneath the Neon Egg* (2014). His stories, essays, translations, and interviews appear regularly in American periodicals. The afterword for this book appeared originally in slightly altered form in *The Writers Chronicle*, May-Summer 2013.